W9-AGI-284

Afghanistan

STEVEN OTFINOSKI

☑®
Facts On File, Inc.

Nations in Transition: Afghanistan

Copyright © 2004 by Steven Otfinoski

Facts On File, Inc.
132 West 31st Street
New York NY 10001

Library of Congress Cataloging-in-Publication Data

Otfinoski, Steven.
  Afghanistan / Steven Otfinoski.
    p.cm.—(Nations in transition)
  Includes bibliographical references and index.
  ISBN 0-8160-5056-2 (alk. paper)
  1. Afghanistan. I. Title. II. Series.
  DS351.5.O86 2003
  958.1—dc21   2003049030

Facts On File books are available at special discounts when purchased in bulk quantities for businesses, associations, institutions, or sales promotions. Please call our Special Sales Department in New York at (212) 967-8800 or (800) 322-8755.

You can find Facts On File on the World Wide Web at
http://www.factsonfile.com

Text design by Erika K. Arroyo
Cover design by Nora Wertz
Map by Jeremy Eagle © Facts On File

Printed in the United States of America

MP JT 10 9 8 7 6 5 4 3 2 1

This book is printed on acid-free paper.

CONTENTS

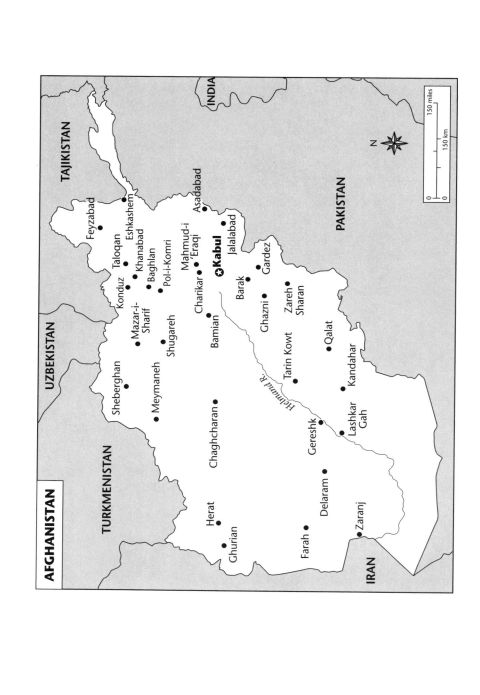

INTRODUCTION

Few Americans knew much about Afghanistan, a remote, impoverished land in Central Asia, before September 11, 2001. They may have recalled that the United States boycotted the 1980 Summer Olympics in Moscow in response to the Soviet Union's invasion of Afghanistan in December 1979. That bitter war decimated Afghanistan and led to the eventual downfall of the Soviet Union.

After September 11, 2001, Afghanistan made front-page news again. The United States was waging a war in Afghanistan, but unlike the countless wars fought in this troubled land, this war was not against the Afghan people but against a tyrannical regime of religious fanatics, the Taliban. The United States was also waging war against the terrorist organization al-Qaeda that had flourished under Taliban rule. It is believed that members of al-Qaeda were responsible for the brutal terrorist attacks on the World Trade Center in New York and the Pentagon in Washington, D.C., in September 2001.

Today, Afghanistan is still very much at the center of world events. Although American forces hunted down and drove out most of the terrorists from Afghanistan, others remain. The conditions that allowed them to thrive there have not been eradicated. Afghanistan remains a desperately poor country with an unstable government. It clings to the past—however bad it was—and goes only reluctantly into the future despite millions of dollars in aid that has poured in from the West to help rebuild and stabilize the country.

To speak of Afghanistan as a "nation" is misleading. Although declared a republic in 1973, after two and a half centuries of monarchy, Afghanistan is still not a unified people under one ruling government. Afghanistan's people are made up of some 20 different ethnic groups, who are further divided into tribes that owe their primary allegiance to a tribal chieftain or warlord. While the tribal system helped the Afghans to defend their land and survive the onslaught of countless invasions, today it is an obstacle to progress.

A Remote and Rugged Land

Another stumbling block to modernization is Afghanistan's harsh geography. Towering mountain ranges, burning deserts, and rolling plains, make travel and communication difficult at best. Some geographers have described Afghanistan as resembling a clenched fist. The comparison is apt for several reasons. Afghanistan's location in southwestern Asia has placed it in the path of countless conquerors and invaders crossing the Asian mainland to India to the south, Russia to the north, and China to the east.

Afghans developed an aggressive stance to fight off these invaders and geography has helped them to do that. The "thumb" of the fist is part of the mountainous plain that extends to the northeast. The midsection of the fist is the central mountain range, the Hindu Kush, an extension of the Himalayan Mountains. And the lower fingers form the southern plateau, mostly made up of arid deserts and semi-deserts.

The mountains have made it difficult for invaders to conquer the people, if not the land itself. They have afforded the Afghans plenty of inaccessible hiding places from which to conduct guerrilla warfare. These same mountains and caves hid retreating Taliban and al-Qaeda fighters in their recent war with the United States.

Afghanistan is about the size of the state of Texas, covering 252,000 square miles (648,000 sq. km). It is bordered on the west by Iran and on the north by the former Soviet republics of Turkmenistan, Uzbekistan and Tajikistan. The northeast tip of Afghanistan touches China, while Pakistan lies to the east and south.

The Northern Plains is made up of high plateaus and grassy hills. It contains Afghanistan's most fertile land. But little of it is arable because of the meager amount of rainfall the region receives. Farms that do exist are found near rivers and in river-fed valleys. Complex irrigation systems have helped to extend cultivation to some extent. A large part of the vast northern grasslands is used for raising and herding sheep and goats.

For centuries, Afghanistan's craggy mountains have been a major obstacle to transportation and communications. This road winds its precarious way through a mountain gorge between Kabul and the Pakistan border. (United Nations)

The Hindu Kush mountain system stretches along the Pakistan border to the east. Its peaks rise to an average of 25,000 feet (7,622 m). The highest point in the country is Nowshak, reaching a height of 24,557 feet (7,487 m). Other mountain ranges are the Paropamisus in the west, which connect to the more central Koh-i-Baba range. Another offspring of the Hindu Kush is the Safed Koh Range, which straddles both Afghanistan and Pakistan. Despite the mountains, the

THE KHYBER PASS

Perhaps the world's most famous mountain pass, the Khyber Pass has been the route of invading armies and the site of bloody battles for centuries.

Surrounded on both sides by craggy cliffs, this mountain pass stretches for about 30 miles and is the best route from eastern Afghanistan to what is now Pakistan (Pakistan was created in 1947; before this, the territory belonged to India). The pass, as narrow as ten feet (3 m) at one point, was used by the conquering armies of Alexander the Great, Tamberlane, Malmed of Ghazni, and others as a route to invade India.

But the Khyber Pass reached its greatest notoriety in the 19th century when the British defended it in order to protect India, their most valuable colony, from attack. It was the scene of many a battle and skirmish during the first two Anglo-Afghan Wars. The British, later on friendlier terms with the Afghans, built a road through the Khyber Pass in 1879. In the 1920s it was modernized into a highway, and a railroad was completed in 1925. The railroad passes through 34 tunnels and over no less than 92 bridges and culverts. Today the Khyber Pass is completely controlled by Pakistan.

central region is the most populous in the country and includes the capital city of Kabul and many smaller cities and towns. It also has the most cultivated land, thanks to the water provided by the Kabul River, which runs eastward into Pakistan. Its many tributaries irrigate the land around Kabul.

The Southern Plateau is dry and arid. It is the least populated region of the country and one of the poorest. It contains such large deserts as the Rīgestān, which covers the southeastern corner of the country. The Darsht-i-Margo and the Dasht-i-Khash are two smaller deserts that lie north of the Helmand River, the longest river in Afghanistan. The Helmand cuts through the heart of the plateau and provides some water for cultivation, but years of drought have made farming difficult at best. To the southwest the desert gives way to the Gawd-i-Zirreh, a marshland, as Afghanistan ends and Iran begins.

A dead tree branch accentuates the desolate beauty of the desert region to the east of Kandahar near the Pakistan border. (Photo courtesy John Otfinoski)

Climate

The climate of Afghanistan is no more inviting than its terrain. The north and south get little precipitation, averaging less than 10 inches a year. The central mountains average up to 15 inches of precipitation, mostly at the lower altitudes. This region is also the most temperate, although the winter months are colder than elsewhere. Average summer temperature in the north and south are 85° to 90° F. In the deserts of the southwest the temperature can soar to 120° F at midday and drop to 32° F, freezing and below at night. But the north can be unbearably hot as well. Here is what one American correspondent experienced in the northern city of Mazar-i-Sharif in June 2001:

> . . . you feel as if you are on another planet. The temperature is usually well over 100 degrees and the wind blows about 40 to 50 miles an hour almost every day, raising huge clouds of dust that hang hundreds of feet

over the desert. You feel as if you're standing in front of a space heater in a dusty attic at the height of summer. Your nostrils fill with dust and dry up; your eyes turn to red slits. You have to wrap a turban around your head and nose and drink a great deal of water. It is a war against desiccation.

While the climate is more pleasant in the mountain altitudes, especially in Kabul and its surrounding area, those areas are also prone to earthquakes. One major earthquake in 1956 killed about 2,000 people. Another natural disaster that frequently strikes in the southwest is sandstorms.

Plants and Animals

Unregulated timber cutting over many generations has left Afghanistan with few forests. The trees that are left on mountainsides, however, are impressive. Large pines and firs rise to 180 feet high. At lower elevations cedar, ash, walnut, oak, and other tree varieties grow. Deodar, a kind of cedar, is the most sought after tree: its timber is used for building houses.

THE AFGHAN HOUND

Afghanistan's most popular animal export is the longhaired Afghan hound. Despite its name, this unique hunting dog originally came from ancient Egypt some 5,000 years ago. But it is the Afghans who bred the dog into an exceptional hunter over the past several centuries.

Standing more than two feet high at the shoulder, the Afghan hound's effectiveness as a hunter comes from its unique anatomy. Its hipbones are higher on its body than almost any other dog breed. This gives it a freedom of movement that makes it extremely swift crossing the rocky, uneven Afghan terrain. Afghan hunters have used it to hunt hares, gazelles, and leopards.

But it is the Afghan hound's richly textured, silky hair and dignified bearing that have made it one of the most prized pet breeds in the West, where it was first introduced after World War I.

Another wildly-popular house pet, the Persian cat, is actually a native of Afghanistan, not Persia (present-day Iran).

Spring is very beautiful in this arid land. It is then that the long-awaited rains cause wildflowers to blossom on the northern mountains slopes and in the grasslands. Cowslip and anemone dominate at this time, while the summer sun helps nurture tall sunflowers, golden marigolds, and sweet-smelling honeysuckle.

Little vegetation thrives in the dry south where date palms dot the desert land and carpets of mint and other herbs flourish.

Unrestricted hunting has largely wiped out the Siberian tiger. Such other large mammals as snow leopards, brown bears, and wolves still roam the mountains, as do large populations of hyenas, foxes, and several types of wild goats and sheep.

The deserts are inhabited by herds of gazelle and the ever-present single-humped dromedaries. The Bactrian camels, which have two humps, reside in the mountains. Both provide an essential means of transportation for nomadic tribes.

Afghan bird life ranges from such large predators as eagles and vultures to game birds, like pheasants and quails, and migratory birds such as herons, pelicans, and sandpipers.

Mountain streams and valley rivers abound with salmon, maki-kholda (a kind of trout), and freshwater crabs. But fishing is not nearly as popular with Afghans as hunting.

One Land, Many Peoples

If the United States and Afghanistan have anything in common, it is the diversity of their populations. The more than 27 million people living in Afghanistan belong to some 20 different ethnic groups, each of which speaks its own language. Most of these groups are further broken down into several tribes, each with its own dialect.

The United States's diversity comes from generations of immigrants. Afghanistan's diversity comes from centuries of invaders. Some members of each wave of invaders settled down and stayed in Afghanistan. Thus the Hazaras are the descendants of the Mongols who invaded Afghanistan in the 13th century. The Uzbeks and Turkmen are the heirs of the Turkish tribes and Tartars who came here from Central Asia.

The so-called "true Afghans," who claim to have lived in this land since early times, are the Pashtuns, also called the Pushtuns or Pashtoons. They are the largest ethnic group, making up nearly 40 percent of the population. According to legend they originally belonged to one of the lost tribes of Israel, tracing their ancestry back to King Saul of the Bible's Old Testament. The Pashtuns are also the most dominant group in Afghanistan. They have traditionally held the highest positions of power in both the military and the government. The last king, Mohammad Zahir Shah (b. 1914), is a Pashtun, as is the current president, Hamid Karzai (b. 1957). Most Pashtuns reside in southeast Afghanistan.

There are two major Pashtun tribes: the Ghilzais, who settled centuries ago near Kandahar, and the Durranis, who were part of the ruling dynasty for nearly two and a half centuries. There is also a large population of Pashtuns in neighboring Pakistan.

The next largest ethnic group is the Tajiks. They make up about 25 percent of the population. They are originally from Persia (now Iran) and are divided into Shi'ites and Sunnis—the two main branches of the religion of Islam. The Shi'ite Tajiks are mostly farmers who live in the mountain villages of Badakhshan and Wakdow. The Sunni Tajiks are middle class city people who work as traders and artisans.

The Hazaras are the third largest ethnic group, making up about 19 percent of the population. Many of them are shepherds in the mountains of central Afghanistan. Others, following the example of their Mongol ancestors, serve in the army, and excel in warfare. The Uzbeks are next in importance, making up 6 percent of the population. They are the largest of the Turkish tribes and are mostly farmers. Smaller tribes include the Turkmen and Kirghiz.

The newest ethnic group, and the most mysterious, is the Nuristanis. They were a fiercely independent tribe living in isolation for centuries in eastern Afghanistan until King Rahman's armies conquered them in 1896 and converted them to Islam. The Nuristanis, mostly farmers and herders, remain largely isolated from other peoples and have strong family ties and ancient traditions.

Finally, there are the nomadic tribes who have followed their sheep, goats, and camels across Afghanistan for centuries. They may form as much as 10 percent of the Afghan population. Nobody knows for certain, however, because they are always on the move and were not counted in the first national census in 1979.

The largest group of nomads is the Kochis, whose population is estimated at 1.5 million. Until recently, they made an annual migration from Afghanistan into Pakistan and back again, trading goods between the two countries. A border dispute between the two countries ended this movement in 1961.

Diversity, which has generally been a positive force in the United States, by making the nation a vital democracy, has not been a positive force in Afghanistan. Ethnic groups identify more closely with their tribes than with the nation of Afghanistan. This tribal mentality has led to countless conflicts and, often, to war. Even today, tribal warlords usually wield more authority in the countryside than does the central government in Kabul.

While diversity has done much to keep Afghans apart, it has also given the country a rich and varied culture. For all their aggression, Afghans are friendly people, who welcome unthreatening strangers. They are courageous, strong, loyal to family and tribal members, and possess a sharp and keen sense of humor. They have needed all these traits to survive a long history in which they have rarely been left alone to live in peace.

NOTE

pp. ix–x "'. . . you feel as if you are . . .'" John Sifton. "Temporal Vertigo," *New York Times Magazine*, September 30, 2001, p. 50.

PART I
History

A CONQUERED LAND (PREHISTORY TO 1919)

"One of the great attractions of the country," said Ted Eliot, former U.S. ambassador in Afghanistan, "was its sense of history." When exactly that history began is not clear, although archaeologists have dug up evidence that an early tribe of hunters inhabited Afghanistan as long as 100,000 years ago. Over time, these people settled down and began growing barley, wheat, and other crops and raising animals for livestock. Villages developed in the north and south, and by about 4000 B.C. they had grown into towns and small cities. The cities traded their grain with people to the south in the Indus Valley of present-day India where the Harappas developed one of the world's first great civilizations.

As other civilizations developed in the Middle East, Central Asia, and the far east, Afghanistan became a crossroads for trade—and war— between other cultures. Wave after wave of invaders left their mark on this land and its people.

Early Invaders

The first to invade and conquer were the Aryans, a people from Central Asia, who moved into Afghanistan about 1500 B.C. Those early Afghan people they did not kill, the Aryans intermarried with, creating a new race.

The Aryans ruled for a thousand years and developed the first distinctive Afghan culture in what became known as Ariana, in present-day northern Afghanistan. Cyrus the Great, founder of the Persian Achaemenian dynasty, invaded Ariana about 540 B.C. and the area became a province, or satrap, of the Persian Empire, known as Bactria. But the Persians fell to a greater conqueror, the Macedonian king Alexander the Great (356–323 B.C.), who defeated them in 330 B.C. at the Battle of Gaugamela. By 328 B.C., Alexander had moved into Afghanistan, capturing the city of Herat near the Persian border and later Kandahar to the south. Alexander was a great admirer of Greek culture, and spread it wherever he went. Evidence of his influence in Afghanistan has been found in the archaeological ruins of a Greek-style city from 325 B.C. at Ay Khanam, which was probably founded by Alexander or his followers.

After Alexander's early death in 323 B.C., the five provinces of Afghanistan came under the rule of one of his generals, Seleucus

Alexander the Great, who conquered Afghanistan in 328 B.C., brought Greek culture to this distant land. (Courtesy Free Library of Philadelphia)

(ca. 354–281 B.C.), who founded the Seleucid dynasty. The Bactrians revolted in 246 B.C. and created their own Graeco-Bactrian kingdom that included the Kabul region and parts of India. It endured for 150 years.

As the new millennium approached, the Kushans, originally from western China, conquered Bactria. The Kushans introduced Buddhism, one of the first of several major religions to be introduced in Afghanistan. As skilled traders they transformed Bactria into one of the great powers in Eurasia, rivaled only by Rome, China, and Parthia, a land in western Asia.

After three centuries of rule, the Kushans declined and fell under the domination of the new Persian dynasty called Sassanid. The Sassanians seized parts of Afghanistan by A.D. 241 and, except for an interim when the Hepthalites of Central Asia took over their lands, remained in power until 642. The Sassanians followed the religion of Hinduism, which began in India, and spread it throughout northern Afghanistan. More evidence of their influence was found recently when a Hindu temple was excavated north of Kabul.

Islam Comes to Afghanistan

But another, new religion would soon sweep across Afghanistan—Islam. Founded in about 613 by the Arabian prophet Muhammad (ca. 570–632), Islam unifies Afghans even today, but that coherence evolved slowly. Islamic armies defeated the Sassanians in 637 at the battle of Qadisiyah, now in present-day Iran, and took over most of Afghanistan by 714. Many of the Islamic dynasties were short-lived and had small power bases. The first great Afghan ruler who created a large and unified kingdom was Mahmud of Ghazna (now Ghazni) (971–1030), son of a former Turkish slave, who came to power in 997 and established his capital at Ghazni, south of Kabul.

Mahmud vowed to invade India every year and probably did so at least 17 times during his reign. His Ghaznavid Empire eventually stretched from northern India to Persia and across Central Asia. He made Ghazni a great center of learning and culture, persuading some of the greatest writers and intellectuals of the Arab world to make their home there. These celebrated figures included the Persian poet Firdausi and the Arab geographer Alberuni.

After Mahmud's death in 1030, the Ghaznavid Empire rapidly declined. The Ghorids of northwestern Afghanistan seized Ghazni and burned it. But greater and fierce conquerors were moving towards Afghanistan from the north.

The Mongol Invasions

The Mongols were great warriors and horsemen from Central Asia who swept across Afghanistan in the early 13th century, led by their great leader Genghis Khan (ca. 1162–1227). The Mongols destroyed Herat and other Afghan cities. Buddhism was literally wiped out by the invaders, but Islam, which had become more entrenched, survived and grew stronger. Much of Genghis Khan's Mongol Empire fell apart on his death in 1227, and local chieftains and lesser Mongol princes took power in a jumble of small city-states.

In China, however, Genghis's grandson, Kublai Khan (1215–1294), ruled over an immense empire. The Venetian merchant and explorer Marco Polo (1254–1324) traveled through Afghanistan in the early 1270s on his way to the court of Kublai Khan. Traveling with his father and uncle, Polo had this to say about Afghanistan and its people:

> In this kingdom there are many narrow defiles [mountain passages], and strong situations, which diminish the apprehension of any foreign power entering it with a hostile intention. The men are good archers and excellent sportsmen; generally clothing themselves with the skins of wild animals; other materials for the purpose being scarce. The mountains afford pasture for an innumerable quantity of sheep, which ramble about in flocks of four, five, and six hundred, all wild; . . . These mountains [the Pamirs] are exceedingly lofty, insomuch that it employs a man from morning till night to ascend to the top of them.

The next great conqueror of Afghanistan was Tamerlane (1336–1405), also known as Timur, a descendant of Genghis Khan. He established the Timurid dynasty by 1370. Unlike Genghis Khan, the Timurids brought culture and learning to the conquered land, rebuilding

Herat to make it their capital and cultural center. The reign of the Timurid dynasty meant a century of peace for Afghanistan (1404–1507)—perhaps its last.

The Moghul Empire

The Timurid golden age ended abruptly when the Turkic Uzbeks, a nomadic people from Central Asia, captured Herat in 1507. But by then power had already shifted to Kabul. The Moghul prince Babur (1483–1530) conquered the area and moved the capital to Kabul in 1504. A descendant of Timur, Babur built the Moghul Empire of India over the next 25 years. In 1526, he moved his capital to Delhi in India, but even after his death eastern Afghanistan remained in the empire he established. The Persians controlled much of the rest of Afghanistan.

In 1709, a Hotaki chieftain, Mirwais Khan (1673–1715), led his people in a revolt against the Persians in Kandahar. Once he'd driven out the Persians, Mirwais Khan became the province's new governor. This national hero began to unite the diverse tribes of Afghanistan, something never attempted before, but died in 1715 before achieving his goal.

An Independent Afghan State and the Durrani Dynasty

Nadir Shah (1688–1747), a member of the Turkish Afghan tribe, made himself the Persian shah, or king, in 1736. He conquered most of Afghanistan, including the region north of the Hindu Kush and was assassinated in 1747. His lieutenant, a Pashtun tribal chief named Ahmad Khan Sadozai (ca. 1722–1772), took power. Ahmad declared an independent Afghan state and spent the next 26 years building a nation out of the conquered provinces and the various tribal clans that inhabited them. He took the title *durr-i-durrani*, meaning "pearl of pearls," and the throne name Ahmad Shah Durrani. The title may have come from the pearl earrings worn by the royal guard of Nadir Shah. The Durrani

MIRWAIS KHAN HOTAKI—AFGHANISTAN'S GEORGE WASHINGTON (1673–1715)

Mirwais Khan Hotaki reigned from 1709–1715 and was Afghanistan's first great national leader and is still admired as one of its greatest heroes.

He was born near Kandahar, the son of a tribal chieftain of the Ghilzai clan of the Hotaks. At the time the Persians of the Safavid Empire dominated southern Afghanistan. At first, Mirwais was a popular local chieftain. Later he was elected mayor of Kandahar. In 1704, the Persians appointed the cruel Gurgin as governor of Kandahar province to keep the rebellious Afghans in check.

Gurgin ruthlessly suppressed the Afghans, imprisoning and executing hundreds of people. Mirwais was arrested on charges of inciting rebellion and was sent to the Persian capital of Isfahan as a prisoner. But the Shah of Persia was deeply impressed by Mirwais and sent him back to Kandahar a free man.

In April 1709, Mirwais invited Gurgin to a picnic at his country home. When the meal ended, he killed the unsuspecting governor and his escort. Then Mirwais led his troops into Kandahar and seized the city. The surprised Persians tried but failed to retake Kandahar.

Mirwais quickly established his power over the entire region, working to unify the Afghan tribes into one fighting force. He sought no great power for himself and refused to accept the title of king in favor of "Baba," meaning father. But he died—of natural causes—before he could establish the unity he so eagerly sought. He was honored in a blue domed mausoleum at the site of his estate at Bagh-i-Kahkan, which remains a national shrine today.

His son, Mahmud, was a tyrant with none of his father's noble qualities. He died within three years of taking the Persian Safavid throne in 1725. Five years later, the rule of the family ended with the rise of the Turkomen Nadir Qoli Beg (later called Nadir Shah).

became Afghanistan's first, and to date, only native dynasty. Ahmad used his power wisely: all decisions were made by a council of chiefs, who represented the various tribes.

When Ahmad died in 1773, no strong ruler came forward to hold the state together. For 45 years his successors and tribal chiefs struggled for power. The empire slowly disintegrated.

The First Anglo-Afghan War

In 1819, the struggle for power in Afghanistan erupted into a civil war that lasted six years. When it was over, a new leader emerged, Dost Mohammad Khan (1793–1863) (see sidebar). He declared himself emir, or prince, and his Barakzay clan ruled Afghanistan into the 20th century.

Dost Mohammad faced new invaders to his land, Great Britain and Russia, the two most powerful nations in Europe. Great Britain wanted Afghanistan in order to protect its most valuable colony, British India, from a northern attack. Russia, seeking to extend its power in Central Asia, wanted to move south through Afghanistan and to gain unchallenged access to the Indian Ocean. The two countries' struggles to control Afghanistan became known as the Great Game.

Dost Mohammad hoped to play the Great Game to Afghanistan's advantage. He asked the British to send aid to help drive the Indian Sikhs out of eastern Afghanistan. When they refused, he turned to the Russians for help. This upset the British, and they decided that Dost Mohammad had to go. British troops invaded Afghanistan in 1839, setting off the First Anglo-Afghan War. They seized the cities of Kandahar and Ghazni. Dost Mohammad fled Kabul and the British installed former king Shah Shuja, who had been living in exile, as their puppet ruler.

The people of Kabul rebelled, forcing the outnumbered British and Indian colonial soldiers to flee (January 6, 1842). A total of about 17,000 soldiers and camp followers sought the safety of a British garrison at Jalalabad, about 90 miles away, pursued by attacking Afghan soldiers. Four days later only about a quarter of the troops were still alive, and, only one person, Dr. Brydon, a British medical officer, survived. It was one of the worst massacres in British military history. Brydon was saved from certain death by a wounded Indian soldier who gave him his mount. "Take my horse and God send you may get to Jalalabad in safety," he told him.

British reinforcements, out for revenge, burned and looted Afghan villages as they marched to Kabul. Once there, they blew up the Great Bazaar, one of the city's most famous landmarks. In April 1842, the hapless Shah Shuja was assassinated. Dost Mohammad was returned to power after the British withdrew from Afghanistan in 1843, bringing the bloody First Anglo-Afghan War to its conclusion.

DOST MOHAMMAD KHAN (1793–1863)

One of the few Afghan rulers to rule twice, Dost Mohammad Khan managed the difficult feat of keeping his country independent during one of the more difficult periods of its modern history.

The son of Payenda Khan, leader of the powerful Barakzay clan, he fought in the civil war that ended in victory for his people. Dost Mohammad became king in 1826 and tried to stay on friendly terms with both Russia and Great Britain, who were battling for control of Afghanistan.

Deposed by the British during the First Anglo-Afghan War, Dost Mohammad lived in exile in India, where he came to admire his aggressors. After returning to power in 1843, he signed peace treaties with the British (1855 and 1857). He also worked diligently to regain control of the outlying regions of his country lost during the war.

In early June 1863 his army, led by his son-in-law, captured Herat from the Iranians who had attacked the city in 1856. Dost Mohammad Khan arrived in Herat only to die there of natural causes on June 9, 1863. It is a tribute to his skills as a leader and negotiator that he remains one of the few Afghan monarchs to have died peacefully in bed.

Afghan king Dost Mohammad Khan surrenders to the British at Kabul during the First Anglo-Afghan War. After the war ended, he returned to power and reigned for another 20 years. (Courtesy Library of Congress)

The Second Anglo-Afghan War

After the death of Dost Mohammad Khan in 1863, his third son came to power. Sher Ali tried to follow his father's example and maintain Afghanistan's independence under continuing pressure from the Russians and British. When he did favor the Russians, preventing a British diplomatic envoy from entering the country in 1878, Britain once again retaliated by declaring war on Afghanistan.

Sher Ali fled north toward Turkestan, but died before he could reach it (1879). His son and successor, Yakub Khan, agreed to concede control of the Khyber Pass and other locations to Britain in order to end the conflict. But when Afghan tribesmen murdered a British envoy, the war heated up again. British troops occupied Kabul and Kandahar. Yakub fled to India and the British put his cousin, Abdur Rahman Khan, in power.

The war taxed British strength. In 1881 they agreed to turn over internal control of the country to Abdur Rahman. However, they retained control of Afghanistan's foreign policy, especially regarding their archenemy in Asia, Russia.

In 1893, with the approval of Abdur Rahman, a grandson of Dost Mohammad Khan, the British established a border between Afghanistan and British India. It was named the Durand Line after the British colonial officer who devised it and was to remain in force for 100 years, even though Afghanistan's legislature never ratified its existence.

Abdur Rahman worked hard to strengthen a weak national government while lessening the traditional power of the tribal chieftains. He encouraged foreign engineers, geologists, and physicians to live in Afghanistan and helped build the country's first small factories that manufactured soap and leather goods. When he died in 1901 Abdur Rahman was succeeded by his son Habibullah Khan (1872–1919).

Reign of Habibullah and World War I

A new century brought many changes to Afghanistan. Habibullah Khan was determined to continue the reforms begun by his father and modernize his backward nation. He kept the peace with the British and concentrated his efforts on internal change. During his nearly two decades of power, Habibullah abolished the practice of slavery, founded new, secular schools, including a Western-style college and a military academy, introduced Western medicine in Afghan hospitals, and established the country's first weekly newspaper. He brought electricity to Afghan cities and towns and encouraged the sales of the first automobiles that were soon rumbling down the streets of Kabul.

Habibullah kept Afghanistan neutral during World War I (1914–1918), which was fought by Great Britain, France, and their Allies against Austria-Hungary and Germany, later joined by the Ottoman Empire of Turkey. Many Afghans, however, supported the Ottomans and wanted to go to war against Great Britain. Habibullah's refusal to do so eventually cost him his life. He was assassinated by Turkish sympathizers while on a hunting trip in 1919, a year after Britain and the Allies won the war.

The Third Anglo-Afghan War and Independence

Habibullah was succeeded by his third son, Amanullah Khan (1892–1960), who did not share his father's strong ties with the British. At his coronation he declared Afghanistan's total independence from Great Britain and immediately launched an attack on British India. This began the third Anglo-Afghan War, the last conflict between the two countries. The British forces were weary after four years of a world war and quickly made peace with the Afghans (August 1919). Under the Treaty of Rawalpindi, which today is located in Pakistan, they granted Afghanistan full independence, with complete control over their own foreign policy. For the first time in two thousand years. Afghans were free of any outside control over their country.

The critical question now was: How would they use this hard-won freedom? Would they move forward and join the growing ranks of the world's modern nations? Or would they remain mired in a past of ignorance, tribal warfare, and division?

NOTES
p. 3 "'One of the great attractions . . .'" *New York Times*, October 21, 2001, Week in Review, p. 2.

p. 6 "'In this kingdom there are many narrow defiles . . .'" Marco Polo. *The Travels of Marco Polo the Venetian.* (Garden City, N.Y.: Doubleday, 1948), pp. 56–57.

p. 9 "'Take my horse and God send you . . .'" "Retreat from Kabul 1842," Afghan War website. Available on-line. URL:http://www.geocities.com/Broadway/Alley/5443/af4.htm. Downloaded on December 4, 2002.

2

THE ROCKY ROAD
TO NATIONHOOD
(1919–1979)

Independence did not end Afghanistan's troubles. Instead it set the stage for struggles between well-meaning, but often autocratic leaders, and reactionary tribal chieftains called warlords. Afghanistan could not build a strong unified nation that equalled European nations in the 20th century. And yet several strong rulers, following the inspired example of Dost Mohammad, did make some strides toward bringing their country into the modern world.

Two Reforming Monarchs

The Bolshevik Revolution of 1917 overthrew the Russian czar and the provisional, democratic government that replaced him. The Bolsheviks were Communists. They transformed Russia and surrounding republics into the Soviet Union. The Soviets were eager to improve relations with their staunch anticommunist Muslim neighbors—especially Afghanistan, because of its continuing value as a buffer state with the British in India.

Amanullah sent an emissary to Moscow in 1919 and Soviet leader, Vladimir Lenin (1870–1924), sent a representative of his government to

Kabul to offer aid to the Afghan government. In May 1921, the Afghans signed a Treaty of Friendship with the Soviets. In the coming years, they supplied Amanullah with money, military equipment, and technology. However, Amanullah did not trust the Soviets any more than he did the British. It was apparent to him that Muslims in the Soviet Union were being oppressed as much as other minorities.

At home, Amanullah pursued a program of rapid reform and modernization. With Soviet assistance he organized an Afghan air force in 1921 and came up with the first national budget in 1922. The following year he proposed and adopted Afghanistan's first constitution. The document called for new laws to replace the old tribal codes, new legislative bodies in the government, and a new unit of currency, the afghani. Three years later, to strengthen his position as Afghan leader, Amanullah changed his title from emir, meaning "prince," to *padshah*, "king."

King Amanullah, seen here in European dress with his cabinet, attempted to drag Afghanistan into the 20th century with a multitude of reforms. Resistance to his reforms eventually led to his abdication and exile in 1929. (Courtesy Library of Congress)

These reforms angered the local warlords. Resistance came to a head in 1928 when Amanullah returned from a European tour, his head full of new ideas. One was to end the age-old exclusion of women from public life. He gave Afghan women the right, if they chose, to no longer wear the veil traditionally worn over their faces. He also established new schools, which both girls and boys could attend. These measures brought the wrath of religious leaders who were opposed to secular education. Uprisings began in eastern Afghanistan and swept across the country. Civil war engulfed Afghanistan. Amanullah abdicated in January 1929 and passed the throne on to his brother Inayatullah. He eventually fled to Europe, where he remained in exile until his death in 1960.

Inayatullah fared no better. He ruled for three days then fled to India. Amid all this turmoil, a Tajik bandit chieftain and people's hero, Bacha

---

MOHAMMED ZAHIR SHAH (b. 1914)

Afghanistan's last king, and one of its longest-ruling monarchs, Mohammed Zahir Shah, was a popular figure. Even 30 years after he was deposed from power, he remains an inspiration for Afghan unity.

He was born in Kabul on October 15, 1914, the son of Muhammad Nader Shah. After his father's assassination in November 1933, 19-year-old Zahir ascended the throne, although real power lay with his three uncles, one of whom became the prime minister. Three decades later Zahir stepped out of the shadows to assert his authority. The 1964 constitution he championed brought some democracy to his troubled country. He even gave up his prerogative as king to give family members public offices.

The Afghan people, however, proved more sensitive to economic issues than political ones. The cycle of drought and famine in the early 1970s that took thousands of lives proved fatal to his government. While Zahir was in Italy undergoing eye surgery, his cousin Mohammad Daoud (1909–78) seized the government. Zahir lived in exile in Italy for the next 30 years.

After much fanfare, the 87-year-old Zahir returned to a free and democratic Afghanistan in April 2002 and was warmly welcomed by

Saqqao, whose name literally meant "Son of the Water Carrier," seized the capital of Kabul. Seeking to legitimatize his rule, Saqqao changed his name to Habibullah Ghazi II. But he remained in power only nine months, after which he was arrested and executed by Amanullah's exiled cousin Muhammad Nader Shah (1883–1933), a descendant of Dost Mohammad.

The tribal council elected Nader Shah the new king. Wanting to avoid his cousin's mistakes, Nader Shah pursued reforms less vigorously. He also created a national army that eventually numbered 40,000 troops. Under Amanullah there had been virtually no standing army. In 1931, Nader Shah also drew up a new constitution that was modeled after Amanullah's constitution in many respects, but was less sweeping in its reforms. Like other Afghan rulers before him, however, Nader Shah allowed no opposition to his rule, and political parties were forbidden. Nonetheless, he managed to unite a fragmented country. He was assassinated in 1933 by a member of a

the Afghan people. Today he is a symbol of a peaceful past and a brighter future for millions of Afghans.

King Zahir Shah, Afghanistan's last monarch, is seen here in exile in Italy in 1987. He finally returned to his homeland in April 2002 to play a role in unifying his country. (AP/ Wide World Photos)

family with whom he had been feuding for years. On Nader Shah's death his son Mohammed Zahir Shah (see sidebar on pp. 16–17), became king.

A Period of Relative Peace

Although Zahir Shah was king, the real power lay in the hands of his uncle, Muhammad Hashim, who was the prime minister. A more skilful politician than the two kings who proceeded him, Hashim was able to slowly begin building a nation. He improved the education system, especially the University of Kabul. He built new highways and supported daily newspapers. He declared Pashtu the official language, an important step in imposing a sense of unity on an extremely divided and diverse population. To avoid problems with the Soviet Union and the United States, Hashim turned to Germany for foreign aid. The Germans helped set up factories and hydroelectric projects in Afghanistan. In 1934, the United States officially recognized Afghanistan as a nation, although the country's continuing friendship with Germany and Italy later caused problems with the Americans as Europe moved towards war.

In 1940, the king proclaimed Afghanistan a neutral country in World War II (1939–45). When Britain and the Soviet Union, who were allies against the Germans, demanded Afghanistan expel nondiplomatic German personnel, the government did so reluctantly. Otherwise, Afghanistan was barely touched by the war. Its neutrality allowed Afghanistan to increase its trade of agricultural products with numerous nations, most notably India.

When the war ended, Afghanistan pursued relations with both the United States and the Soviet Union. The cold war that developed in the late 1940s between the two superpowers forced Afghanistan to the sidelines. It refused to commit itself to one country or the other.

Trouble with Pakistan

Afghanistan, however, could not avoid conflict with a new neighbor, Pakistan. In 1947, India won its independence from Great Britain and

Indian Muslims demanded an independent state of their own from the Hindu majority. This is how Pakistan came into being. Afghan Pashtuns living on the Pakistan frontier demanded that they be allowed to establish their own state, "Pashtunistan," that would be independent of Pakistan. To facilitate this, they disputed the Durand Line, Afghanistan's border with Pakistan, which the Afghans never officially recognized. Pakistan refused to change the boundary line and closed its borders with Afghanistan. This quarrel over a homeland for Pakistan's Pashtuns would remain unresolved for decades.

The First Reign of Mohammad Daoud

Muhammad Hashim's youngest brother, Shah Mahmud, replaced him as prime minister in 1946. Under his government, the Helmand Valley Project, an ambitious irrigation program for southwestern Afghanistan, was begun, largely with financial aid from the United States.

In 1953, Mohammad Daoud (1909–78), who was also the king's cousin and brother-in-law, succeeded his uncle, Shah Mahmud, as prime minister. A strong leader, Daoud began a cautious but ambitious national

Prime Minister Mohammad Daoud started new reforms in the 1950s to modernize Afghan life. The women in the picture are no longer forced by law to wear the body-length burka. *However, only one of them has chosen not to wear it.* (United Nations)

program for modernization. To fund his projects, he collected foreign aid from both the United States and the Soviet Union. He granted more rights to Afghan women and called for the voluntary removal of the veil. Daoud improved roads, and built factories to increase Afghanistan's modest industrial output. He also built hydroelectric plants to distribute cheap energy to towns and villages.

In 1955, Soviet leaders Nikita Khrushchev (1894–1971) and Nikolay Bulganin visited Kabul and offered Daoud a $100 million development loan. The same year the Soviets and their allies gave Afghanistan $25 million in military aid. These growing ties with the Soviets would have serious consequences for Afghanistan in the years ahead.

MOHAMMAD DAOUD KHAN (1909–1978)

A strong leader with strong opinions, Mohammad Daoud Khan made lasting contributions to his country. But, like so many other Afghan rulers his inability to share power eventually led to his downfall.

His father, Muhammed Aziz Khan, served as Afghan foreign minister from 1917 to 1919. He died in 1933 in Berlin, Germany. Daoud, and his cousin King Zahir Shah, were dominated by the older generation of their clan, namely their three powerful uncles. When Daoud took over as prime minister in 1953 a new generation of leaders brought fresh ideas and a new outlook to their country.

Daoud's quarrel with Pakistan president Ayub Khan (1907–1974) ruptured diplomatic relations between the two countries. The loss of trade with Pakistan hurt the Afghan economy and eventually led to Daoud's fall from power. When a decade later, he came back to power, Daoud pursued new unsettling policies. He turned away from both the United States and the Soviet Union. He forged relations and alliances with other Islamic nations. He opposed government ownership of businesses that he had pursued when he had been trying to gain the support of the growing People's Democratic Party of Afghanistan (PDPA). He encouraged private enterprise which angered the PDPA and which eventually led to the coup that murdered him.

It was not Daoud's relations with the Soviets that got him into trouble at home, however. Many Afghans were critical of his obsession with the establishment of Pashtunistan and his ongoing disagreements with the Pakistanis. They wanted Daoud to pay closer attention to the economy, which was in decline. King Zahir Shah finally asserted himself and forced his cousin to resign as prime minister in 1963.

A Constitutional Monarchy

Within two weeks of his cousin's resignation, Zahir appointed a commission to draw up a new constitution. In the spring of 1964, he called for a *loya jirgah*, a national assembly, to meet and approve the constitution. By September, the new constitution was law.

The 1964 constitution was a landmark in modern Afghan history and a model for other Asian nations. Under it, Afghanistan became a constitutional monarchy. This meant that the king still ruled, but his acts had to be approved by the democratic legislature consisting of two bodies— the House of the People and the House of the Elders. The House of the People would be fully elected by Afghan voters. The House of the Elders, the upper house, would be partially elected and partially appointed by the king.

When elections were held in 1965, Afghan women were allowed to vote for the first time. Four legislative seats went to members of the newly-formed People's Democratic Party of Afghanistan (PDPA), a pro-Communist, pro-Soviet political group. One of the four elected was Nur Mohammad Taraki, who, with Babrak Karmal (b. 1929), led the PDPA. The two leaders later split over personal differences.

What Zahir did not bargain for was strong opposition from the very legislature he helped form. Because of this, the government was stalemated on many issues. As for the majority of the Afghan people, they were not used to representative government and failed to support it fully. The king did not have the popular power base he had hoped for to change and modernize Afghan society. His government was further weakened by a series of severe droughts that struck the country in the early 1970s and left thousands dead from starvation.

The Return of Daoud Khan

In 1973, Daoud Khan led a military coup and seized the government. Unlike most coups in Afghanistan's history, this one was bloodless. King Zahir abdicated. Daoud abolished the monarchy, sent the king into exile, and declared Afghanistan a republic. But it was a republic in name only because Daoud, as both president and prime minister, ruled the country like a dictator. He dissolved the legislature and outlawed all political parties.

Daoud renewed relations with the Soviet Union and signed a 10-year, Soviet-Afghan Treaty of Neutrality and Non-Aggression in 1975. This action disturbed Afghanistan's Muslim majority who did not want atheistic Communists holding power over them. As a result, Daoud attempted to distance his government from the Soviets, but this angered the PDPA and other leftist groups. When he tried to purge the military of leftist officers, they struck back.

Removed from power in 1963, Mohammad Daoud returned to office in 1973, ousting the man who had earlier ousted him, his cousin King Zahir Shah. (AP/Wide World Photos)

The April Revolution and Its Aftermath

On April 27, 1978, the Great Saura, or April Revolution, took place. It was led by high-ranking leftist military officers. They took over the capital and killed Daoud, his family, and hundreds of his followers. Eight leaders of the PDPA were released from prison and assumed power. They renamed the country the Democratic Republic of Afghanistan (DRA) and elected Taraki president and prime minister. Taraki proved himself a brutal and tactless leader. He forced a Communist way of life on a mostly devout Muslim nation, formed stronger economic ties with the Soviets, and even changed the Afghan flag so that its colors matched those of the Soviet Union's flag. Taraki's grand plans for the redistribution of land to the poor found little support among the people. Within a year, he was overthrown and suffocated to death on the orders of his own vice-president, Hafizullah Amin.

Amin assumed power and proved to be a greater tyrant than Taraki. He used his private police force, the National Organization for the Defense of the Revolution, to ruthlessly oppress the people. Muslim opposition continued to grow and a rebel movement was born. The Soviet Union feared a civil war would erupt and that the unstable Afghan government would not be able to quell it.

Meanwhile, Amin accused the United States of undermining his government and providing aid to the rebels. In late 1979, U.S. ambassador Adolph Dubs was kidnapped by Afghans and later murdered. The United States immediately cut all aid to the country.

As the situation worsened, the Soviet Union urged Amin to moderate his Marxist policies to gain the support of the people, but he stubbornly refused. The Soviets quietly built up their troop force at the Afghan border in the north. Then on Christmas Day, 1979, Soviet troops crossed the border and invaded Afghanistan. What might have been a civil war was now far more complicated by the Soviets' intervention. Once more Afghanistan was about to enter a long and bloody period of war and destruction.

3

THE NEW INVADERS—THE SOVIETS, THE TALIBAN, AND AL-QAEDA (1979 TO THE PRESENT)

The Soviets justified their invasion of Afghanistan as necessary to support and aid the legitimate Communist government in Kabul. In actual fact, they wanted to create a puppet state that would be controlled by Moscow and serve as a buffer between them and the nations of Pakistan and India. Their true motives became clear when the less-than-malleable Amin was overthrown and killed in a Soviet-inspired coup two days after the invasion began. Soviet-trained deputy prime minister Babrak Karmal, who had fallen out with Amin and had been living in exile in Moscow, was parachuted into the country by Soviet transport. The same day Amin was killed, Karmal was declared the new president of Afghanistan.

The Afghan army was unable to keep order or secure the stability of the unpopular Karmal administration. More and more Soviet troops were brought in to buttress the president and keep at bay the millions of Afghans who opposed him. Feeble attempts to broaden the Karmal government's power base failed miserably. The Soviets had not counted on the stubborn resistance of the Afghan people to foreign domination, their grim perseverance in the face of hardship, and their total devotion to their Islamic faith, now under attack by godless communism.

Rise of the Mujahideen

The Muslim tribes of Afghanistan formed guerrilla groups to fight the Soviets and the Afghan army. They gradually organized a resistance movement, headed by local warlords who put aside their differences to fight a common enemy. They called themselves the mujahideen, which means "holy warriors" in English. In 1985, those who followed the Sunni branch of Islam formed the Islamic Union of Afghan Mujahideen (IUAM). Two years later the Shi'ite Muslims formed a similar group, the Islamic Coalition Council of Afghanistan (ICCA), with headquarters in neighboring Iran.

The various mujahideen groups fought the Soviets with the same guerrilla tactics that their ancestors had used successfully for centuries. Small groups of fighters would attack a Soviet installation with lightning speed and then melt away into the mountains, where pursuit was difficult. While vastly outnumbered by a Soviet force of from 90,000 to 104,000 troops at any one time, the mujahideen had the advantage of surprise and an intimate knowledge of the landscape. They were further aided by military supplies and weapons provided by the United States, China, and Pakistan, all of whom condemned the Soviet invasion as an act of aggression.

Here is the description of a typical Afghan ambush on Soviet troops by two former Soviet military officers:

> Participants . . . took position along a road at a distance of about two hundred meters [656 ft.], separated from one another by about thirty meters [98 ft.]. When the Soviet column entered the killing zone, the rebels directed fire first at vehicle drivers and command personnel. Then they began to fire at trucks carrying personnel. Simultaneously, grenade launchers were fired at armored vehicles escorting the convoy.

The Soviets continued to fight in the air with jets and helicopters and on land with tanks, artillery, and armed personnel carriers. As the

AHMED SHAH MASSOUD (1956–2001)

Of all the heroes of the mujahideen, none were as charismatic as or displayed greater leadership abilities than Ahmad Shah Massoud.

He was born in the tiny village of Bazarak in the Panjshir Valley in the Hindu Kush mountains, the son of a senior army officer. Young Massoud was attending college when the Soviet invasion took place in December 1979. It was a defining moment in his life. Massoud left school and headed for the mountains to join the growing resistance against the Communists. After several successful campaigns, Massoud emerged as one of the most effective commanders of the mujahideen in fighting the Soviets. He was known as "the Lion of Panjshir," named for the place which was his home and headquarters.

After the Soviets withdrew, Massoud became one of the leaders of the new Rabbani government, serving as defense minister. When the Taliban seized Kabul, Massoud and his comrades returned to the mountains to fight once more. In 1999, Massoud helped form the Northern Alliance, a group of mujahideen groups that fought the Taliban.

Massoud was in the process of waging a major campaign against the Taliban, when he was interviewed, on September 9, 2001, along with a number of other leaders of the Northern Alliance, by what they thought were two television journalists. In fact, the pair were agents of Osama bin Laden, leader of the terrorist group, al-Qaeda. One of the two terrorists set off a bomb, hidden in his camera, killing himself and Massoud. That was two days before the terrorists attacked the World Trade Center and the Pentagon in the United States.

On the brink of change, Afghanistan lost the man many expected to lead them into a new era. "His mission in life was the freedom of Afghanistan, and he became a martyr for that cause," eulogized President Harmid Karzai at a memorial service to commemorate the first anniversary of Massoud's death. "We will continue to fulfill the objectives and desires of the man who lies buried here."

fighting in the countryside intensified, many Afghans fled their villages and towns and sought refuge in Kabul, which was relatively secure and peaceful. Many more fled the country, settling temporarily in Pakistan or Iran.

An Unpopular War

As the war dragged on, more and more Soviet troops were sent to Afghanistan, and the number of casualties rose. By the war's end in 1988, about 15,000 Soviet soldiers had been killed in the fighting. Other casualties numbered nearly 470,000, the majority of whom suffered from infectious disease, caused by poor diet and sanitation. The Soviet people began to question why their sons were being killed and wounded in a foreign country. The war was expensive as well, hurting the already unstable Soviet economy. Also, Soviet relations with other Muslim countries were deteriorating.

Soviet leader Leonid Brezhnev (1906–1982) who had initiated the war, died in 1982 of a heart attack. He was succeeded by two equally aged men, Yuri Andropov and Konstantin Chernenko, both of whom died within about a year of taking office. In 1985, Mikhail Gorbachev (b. 1931), a younger, pragmatic politician came to power in the Kremlin. He called the costly war in Afghanistan "a bleeding wound" and sought to take steps to de-escalate it. In 1986, he ordered 8,000 troops to withdraw and agreed to participate in negotiations in Geneva, Switzerland, led by the United Nations (UN). The mujahideen's refusal to participate in the negotiations and the Soviet's reluctance to withdraw more troops from Afghanistan slowed down efforts to end the war.

Najibullah Takes Over

In May 1986, Babrak Karmal was replaced as secretary general by the former head of the government's secret police, Major General Mohammad Najibullah (1947–1996). Trained and supported by the Soviet secret police, the KGB, Najibullah attempted to rally more of the population behind his government. In November 1987 he drafted a new constitution that called for the participation in government of non-Communist political parties. The country's name was changed back to the Republic of Afghanistan, a symbolic gesture that failed to appease the freedom fighters. On their part, the Soviets called for a six-month unilateral cease-fire, but the resistance leaders refused to honor it.

The morale of the Afghan army was reaching an all-time low. The army had shrunk from over 100,000 fighters at the start of the war to less than 25,000. Many Afghans drafted into the army deserted at the first opportunity. Morale was also low among Soviet troops, and anti-war feelings at home were intensifying. Gorbachev knew he had to end the war or lose face in a Soviet Union that was already cracking at the seams from decades of misrule and corruption.

The End of One War

On April 14, 1988, a peace agreement was signed between the Soviets and Afghan representatives. Under the agreement the Soviets would withdraw all troops and leave Afghanistan a neutral state. The mujahideen, however, refused to sign the agreement and pledged to continue to fight. Nevertheless, Soviet troops began to withdraw a month

An Afghan woman walks past a Soviet army officer who keeps a watch from a Soviet checkpoint in downtown Kabul on April 25, 1988. (AP/Wide World Photos/Liu Heung Shing)

later. It was the first time in 300 years that the Afghans had driven a foreign army from their homeland.

But the civil war between the Communist government of Najibullah and the mujahideen continued unabated. For seven months, the rebels lay siege to Jalalabad, near the Pakistan border. Ten thousand fighters died and still the mujahideen failed to take the city. However, without the Soviets to prop him up, Najibullah's power was weakening. In May 1990 he tried to set up a multiparty system, but the mujahideen continued to fight him. Even after the United States stopped sending weapons and other military aid the following year, the fighting went on.

In early 1992, mujahideen leader Ahmad Shah Massoud joined forces with Uzbek warlord General Abdul Rashid Dostum to form the Northern Alliance, a military coalition dedicated to bringing down Najibullah's government.

An Uneasy Peace

The Northern Alliance marched on Kabul in April 1992. Najibullah resigned as president on April 16, ending 14 years of Communist rule and internal warfare. In that time more than 2 million Afghans had died and 5.5 million had fled the country. Half a million farm animals had been killed, and 100,000 acres of forest destroyed. Agriculture had been disrupted in the fighting, and a famine swept many areas, forcing people to flee their villages or face death by starvation.

But with the long war over, the various warlords had no reason to stay united. They quarreled and jockeyed for power. The age-old rivalry of the Pashtuns and the Tajiks, the two largest ethnic groups, resurfaced. Burhanuddin Rabbani (b. 1940), a former professor of Islamic law at Kabul University and the leader of the Islamic Society of Afghanistan (ISA), was named interim president on June 28, 1992. In December the ethnic Tajik was elected to a full term by the tribal leaders.

By mid-1993, the Northern Alliance unofficially fell apart. About the same time those Afghans who had fled their country were beginning to return home. Some 120,000 refugees came from Tajikistan, the former Soviet republic to the north. But the homeland they returned to was not the land they had known before the Soviet invasion. It was filled with tribal tension. If this was peace, it was very fragile.

Renewed Civil War

The New Year of 1994 got off to an ominous start when two former Northern Alliance leaders, Hekmatyar and Dostum, attacked Kabul. Over the next six months 2,500 people were killed.

While civil war raged, the nation's economy worsened. Farmers fled their villages for the cities, the fields remained fallow. Ten million dollars in aid from the UN for food and medicine could only begin to meet the country's needs. By the end of the year the death toll from the civil war had risen to 7,000, with about 100,000 injured and 500,000 left homeless. Hekmatyar and Dostum's forces failed to take Kabul, but their long effort seriously hurt Rabbani's power.

Rise of the Taliban

Among the political and religious factions that sprung up in this turbulent time was an obscure group of extreme fundamental religious teachers of Pashtun background from the rural area surrounding the southern city of Kandahar. They called themselves "the Mosquitoes of Islam," but to others they were the Taliban, a group whose name means religious students. "Islamic faith is a bright light; we seem to be so close to it that we catch fire," said their leader, former freedom fighter in the war against the Soviets, Mullah Muhammad Omar (see sidebar).

Like a slowly spreading flame, the Taliban began to sweep across the south and in October 1994, much to the surprise of the country's other factions, they seized control of Kandahar.

Well organized and with the single-mindedness of true believers, the Taliban began to build their forces in southern Afghanistan. Many Afghans found Islamic fundamentalism appealing, and the Taliban's call for law and order a righteous one. Compared to the selfish, power-driven warlords, the Taliban seemed like saints.

MULLAH MUHAMMAD OMAR (b. 1962)

One of the most mysterious men in modern Afghan history, Mullah Muhammad Omar controlled Afghanistan for six years with his unique brand of Islamic extremism, social righteousness, and religious mysticism. The date and place of his birth is disputed, but many believe he was born to poor Pashtun peasants in 1962 in a village near Kandahar. He became a freedom fighter during the Soviet war and was blinded in one eye by shrapnel during the 1980s. When the Soviets withdrew in 1989, Omar became a crusading vigilante, fighting corruption and the abuse of women. He became famous after he caught a man who raped a girl and hanged him from a tank barrel.

Largely uneducated despite some university training in Pakistan, Omar joined other right-wing Islamic teachers in the mid-1990s to form the Taliban. After the Taliban took Kabul in 1996, they elected him the Leader of the Faithful. Mullah Omar (*mullah* refers to a religious, educated Muslim leader) was a strong, but elusive leader who has never, to anyone's knowledge, allowed his photograph to be taken. During the Taliban's reign, he rarely left his headquarters in Kandahar and let his foreign minister be his public voice.

Omar's ties to his old friend from the Soviet days, terrorist Osama bin Laden (see sidebar), eventually brought down his regime, but his whereabouts in May 2003 was still unknown. While he is at large, he remains a threat to the future security of the new, democratic Afghanistan.

In a rare interview for the Voice of America shortly before the Americans attacked his country, Omar boasted: "Even if it [the United States] were twice as strong or twice that, it could not be strong enough to defeat us. We are confident that no one can harm us if God is with us."

The UN tried to oversee negotiations to end the civil strife in Afghanistan in February 1995. Their objective was to turn over power in Kabul to a council of representatives of all ethnic and political groups. Rabbani agreed to step down as president, and a council was elected, but the Taliban refused to participate, calling the council corrupt.

By September 1995, Taliban forces took over Herat, the key city in the west. A year later they were marching on Kabul, which soon surrendered. Mujahideen leader Ahmad Shah Massoud and Rabbani and their followers fled north to Mazar-i-Sharif, when they would resurrect the Northern Alliance to fight the Taliban. Left behind was former Communist leader Najibullah, who Taliban soldiers dragged out of the palace and hanged in the street along with his brother. Now in control of most of the country, the Taliban declared Afghanistan a "completely Islamic state."

A Brutal Regime

At first, most Afghans welcomed Taliban rule. They cracked down hard on crime and corruption and made the streets and byways safe for the first time in more than 20 years. But there was a high price to be paid for this order. As Islamic extremists, the Taliban's interpretation of Islamic law was rigid and unyielding. Women, many of whom had been working in various jobs and professions, who were well educated, and accustomed to Western clothes, were sent home and told to stay there. They were only

An anti-Taliban soldier expresses his sense of loss at the destruction of a price-less Buddha statue by the Taliban in August 2002. The statue stood in the now empty niche in the rock face. (AP/Wide World Photos/Wally Santana)

allowed to venture into public wearing a *burka*, a garment that covered their bodies from head to toe, and accompanied by a male relative. Men were ordered to grow beards long enough to extend out of a closed fist. Dancing and music, considered sinful, were strictly forbidden, as were such innocent pastimes as chess and kite flying.

Books considered irreligious or which espoused Western ideas were shot to pieces by Taliban soldiers. Art works depicting the human body were destroyed. The most lamentable example of Taliban censorship may have been their destruction of two 1,500-year-old statues of Buddha chiseled into a cliff in the central Bamiya Valley. Because these priceless pre-Islamic antiquities depicted the human form they were deemed idolatrous by the Taliban. The United Nations Educational, Scientific and Cultural Organization (UNESCO) pleaded with the Taliban to spare the artworks and even sent a special envoy to negotiate with them. But in March 2001, the Buddhas were destroyed with jackhammers. "The destruction by the Taliban of the pre-Islamic statuary . . . is a dreadful loss for the memory of mankind," said UNESCO director general Koichiro Matsuurra.

In Afghanistan, anyone who broke the Taliban's draconian laws was harshly punished. "In October [1996], one woman had the tip of her thumb cut off for wearing nail varnish and another was whipped with a car antenna for letting her *burkha* slip. . . ." wrote one foreign correspondent. "A man who had chosen not to pray was taken to the street called *Kafir*, meaning godless, and executed."

Many others accused of breaking Taliban law were executed before 20,000 to 30,000 spectators in the National Stadium in Kabul.

These tyrannical tactics were roundly condemned by the West. For women, daily life amounted to constant torture. They were forbidden from speaking to men who were not blood relatives, forbidden from making noise when they walked, and forbidden even from being visible through a window in their own home. A woman and man caught committing adultery would be stoned to death.

Afghan women lived in constant fear for their lives. A woman named Floran tells of her experiences under the Taliban:

Once I went shopping with my sister. The weather was warm and I couldn't take a breath under my veil. I said to my sister that I wanted to raise my veil for a minute. She had forbidden me to do that. So when we reached an alley, we both raised our veils assuming that the Taliban were not there. A few minutes later we heard a terrible voice that echoed to our ear that "aren't you ashamed showing your faces to strangers?" We both stopped and begin to shiver. . . . I think that we are the most unlucky and ill-fated women of the world.

The American ambassador to the UN attempted to broker peace talks with the Taliban, but they quickly fell apart. In March 1998, the UN withdrew its staff from Kandahar and four months later two UN staff members were murdered in Jalalabad.

The al-Qaeda Connection

One of the most disturbing aspects of the Taliban government was its support of the Arab terrorist organization al-Qaeda and its leader, the notorious Osama bin Laden. Bin Laden had been generally believed to be the mastermind behind several major acts of terror in the 1990s, including the bombing of American embassies in Kenya and Tanzania in August 1998 that killed more than 220 people. Mullah Omar, the Taliban's leader in Afghanistan, was connected to al-Qaeda for economic reasons as much as for ideological ones. Bin Laden was the heir to a Saudi oil fortune and paid the Taliban government millions to allow him to operate in their country.

Seeking to bring bin Laden to justice, the United States offered a $5 million reward for information that would lead to his capture. In 1997, it began to put pressure on the Taliban government to turn over bin Laden, who was known to be operating terrorist training camps in Afghanistan. In November of that year, after months of stalling, the Taliban agreed to try bin Laden on charges of terrorism. They promptly found him innocent. In February 1998, they declared that bin Laden had "disappeared."

Angry and frustrated, the United States and the UN imposed trade sanctions and weapons embargoes on Afghanistan through the summer and fall of 1999. When the *USS Cole*, an American battleship stationed in Yemen, was sabotaged on October 12, 2000, and 17 U.S. servicemen killed, the United States threatened to attack Afghanistan if bin Laden was found to be behind the bombing.

But as the year 2000 came to close, few Americans were concerned about events in Afghanistan. Their attention was focused on the most delayed outcome of a U.S. election in 100 years, from which Republican George W. Bush (b. 1946) finally emerged as the surprise victor (he was inaugurated on January 20, 2001). Afghanistan and its problems seemed remote to America. All that changed nine months later on a beautiful late summer morning in New York City.

September 11 and Its Aftermath

At 8:48 A.M. an American Airlines passenger jet, hijacked by terrorists after leaving Boston's Logan Airport, careened into the North Tower of the nation's second tallest structure, the World Trade Center (WTC) in Lower Manhattan. Fifteen minutes later a second hijacked jet struck the WTC's South Tower. At 9:37 A.M., a third hijacked plane crashed into the Pentagon building in Washington, D.C. A fourth hijacked jet, headed for Washington (and possibly the White House), crashed into a field near Shanksville, Pennsylvania, at 10:10 A.M., when the passengers overwhelmed the hijackers. By 10:30, both WTC towers, engulfed in flames, had collapsed. Nearly 3,000 people died in the four locations. It was one of the worst days in U.S. history and the most terrible act of terrorism ever committed on American soil.

The U.S. government believed—a belief later confirmed—that Osama bin Laden and al-Qaeda were behind these heinous acts. President George W. Bush, with much of the international community behind him, gave the Taliban an ultimatum—turn over bin Laden or prepare to be attacked. Mullah Omar refused, claiming to believe— according to an interview with a former member of his household—that the United States was using its hunt for bin Laden as a pretext to destroy the Taliban.

The United States Attacks

On October 1, less than three weeks after the attacks in New York and Washington, the United States, assisted by Great Britain and Australia,

OSAMA BIN LADEN (b. 1957–   )

Although not an Afghan, Osama bin Laden has helped to turn this country into a breeding ground for international terrorism. He is the most wanted fugitive in United States history.

Osama bin Laden was born in Saudi Arabia in 1957, the 17th of 24 sons of an immigrant bricklayer from Yemen. Through hard work and a sharp business sense, bin Laden's father became one of the wealthiest building contractors in the country.

When bin Laden was about 12, his father died in an airplane crash and he inherited a huge fortune. As a youth, he was a pious Muslim. But as a civil engineering student at King Abdul Aziz University, he gained a reputation as a playboy who preferred women and drink to his studies. The Soviet invasion of Afghanistan in 1979 was a turning point in bin Laden's life. He felt solidarity with the Afghans and gave millions of his money to support the mujahideen.

In 1984, bin Laden moved to Pakistan where he worked closely with the radical Muslim extremist Abdullah Azzam. His hatred of the Soviets soon extended to all Western countries that interfered with Muslim nations, including the United States. In 1986, he established a training camp for terrorists. Two years later he founded al-Qaeda (meaning "the Base"), with the Egyptian terrorist group Islamic Jihad (Holy War). He returned briefly to Saudi Arabia in 1989, but then moved back to Afghanistan and then to the Sudan in Africa. The Saudis revoked his citizenship in 1994, a year after terrorists were credited with the bombing of an underground garage at the World Trade Center. Many believed bin Laden was the mastermind behind this and other terrorist acts in the 1990s.

The United States pressured the Sudan to expel bin Laden in 1996, and he returned to Afghanistan where, under the Taliban, he found a safe haven and developed a large terrorist training program.

Following the second bombing of the World Trade Center and the attacks on the Pentagon on September 11, 2001, and the subsequent defeat of the Taliban by American forces, bin Laden has gone into hiding. For a time there were rumors that he had died. But a tape of his voice, released in November 2002, led most experts to believe that Osama bin Laden is still alive.

began bombing Afghanistan. President Bush declared that the U.S. was at war with the Taliban and not the Afghan people. Over the next month, American B-52s and other aircraft dropped up to 10,000 bombs on the country. Although measures were taken to avoid hitting civilian targets, a Red Cross building was bombed twice and innocent civilians were killed.

Taliban resistance was strong at first, but quickly buckled. Never a highly disciplined army, the Taliban troops, many of them conscripts, swiftly lost the will to fight. While the Taliban leaders fought on grimly, their foot soldiers surrendered readily to the United States and their ally, the Northern Alliance.

"The Taliban were not from the masses," explained Sabir Latifi, an Afghan businessman. "They were like a raft on the river. They had no roots."

Uprooting the Taliban was relatively easy, but al-Qaeda was another matter. The terrorists hid in the rugged mountains, and often in caves. The only way U.S. combat units could flush them out was to fight them, cave by cave. Osama bin Laden eluded capture, although several of his lieutenants were captured or killed. Eventually many of the surviving al-Qaeda terrorists fled across the border, supposedly into northern Pakistan where they had many sympathizers.

This illustration is from a propaganda leaflet dropped over Afghanistan by the U.S. Department of Defense in response to the terrorist attacks of September 11, 2001. It depicts Taliban members trapped in caves by U.S. missiles. In a short time this fiction would become reality as the United States launched a full-scale attack on the Taliban government. (Courtesy Library of Congress)

On November 9, 2001, the city of Mazar-i-Sharif fell to the forces of the Northern Alliance. Within days, their troops were marching into Kabul. The Taliban was in retreat and only retained control over Kandahar. That too fell in a matter of weeks. While many members of the Taliban government were captured and imprisoned, their leader, Mullah Muhammad Omar, escaped.

A New Beginning

The relief felt throughout Afghanistan was immediate and infectious. The terrible rule of the Taliban had been lifted and the populace rejoiced in its newfound freedom. Courageous women appeared in public without their long *burkor*. Men lined up at barbershops to have their beards shaved. But once the initial celebration ended, it was time to begin rebuilding a devastated country after more than two decades of harsh rule, war, and displacement.

On December 11, 2001, Afghan leaders and Western advisers met in Bonn, Germany, to draw up a charter. It called for an interim government to be appointed for six months, when an Afghan grand assembly, called a *loya jirga*, would elect a provisional government that would serve for two years. At the end of that time, a full-term parliamentary government would be chosen in national elections. Hamid Karzai (b. 1957) (see chapter 5 sidebar), a 44-year-old nationalist who had the support of the United States, was appointed interim chairman for six months.

Despite his popularity with the Americans, Karzai was something of an outsider in Afghan affairs. He last held public office in 1992, when he had served as deputy foreign minister in the Rabbani government. Karzai was not part of the Northern Alliance leadership, made up mostly of Tajiks, the second-largest ethnic group in the country. His elegant Western dress and fine education made many ordinary Afghans suspicious of him.

Karzai assured the people that he would represent all of them in his government. "Let us be good to each other and be compassionate and share our grief," he said in a speech on the occasion of his swearing in, "Let us forget the sad past."

But the past was still very much alive in Afghanistan. The hunt for al-Qaeda and Osama bin Laden continued, led by more than 4,500 U.S.

troops and other international peacekeepers. A number of the warlords, many of them associated with the Northern Alliance, were busy rebuilding their own forces in the countryside, posing a potential threat to the central government in Kabul.

Karzai successfully raised millions of dollars in aid by traveling abroad to meet with officials in supportive Western nations. In January 2002, the United States pledged $296 million in reconstruction aid, in addition to the $400 million President Bush already committed for humanitarian aid. This was only, however, a small percent of the $17 billion in aid that the UN said was needed for Afghanistan's first year of freedom.

Karzai Is Elected President

On June 13, 2002, more than 1,500 elected delegates from all ethnic groups and regions arrived in Kabul to take part in the *loya jirga* (see sidebar, chapter 5), an Afghan tradition for more than 250 years.

The delegates elected Karzai interim president by an overwhelming majority. A National Assembly of 160 members was also elected by the delegates. Since first coming to power, Karzai had proven his leadership abilities and now enjoyed the support of most of the population. However, the problems his new government face seem incredibly daunting. The government's authority, is still largely limited to Kabul. A national army is being trained by American and French troops. So far, it has only 3,000 soldiers. The goal is to have 9,000 to 12,000 soldiers by the summer of 2004. Karzai eventually hopes to have a national army of 70,000 strong.

Even with millions of dollars in aid, there are few government resources to relieve widespread hunger, disease, and poverty. Besides this, Karzai remains a minority within his own government. While he is Pashtun, a majority of his ministers are Tajik.

Assassinations and Set Backs

A series of violent acts over the next several months called the government's stability into question. On February 14, 2001, while Karzai was still provisional leader, Abdul Raham, the minister of aviation and tourism, was beaten to death by a mob at Kabul Airport. His death may have been related to his strong support for the return of King Zahir, which was opposed by the powerful Tajiks in the government. They feared that his presence would be a rallying point for Pashtuns, a majority in the country, but a minority in the government.

On July 6, 2002, Vice President Haji Abdul Qadir, one of the few Pashtuns in the government, was shot to death by two gunmen as he arrived at his office (as of May 2003, his killers remained at large). Less than two months later, on September 5, 2002, President Karzai himself narrowly escaped assassination while attending a brother's wedding in Kandahar. Three hours later, a car bomb went off in Kabul, killing 30 people and injuring 170 others. Both acts have been attributed to al-Qaeda. It seemed no place in the country was completely safe and secure from the terrorists and their supporters.

Karzai refused to let the attempted assassination stop his plans in Kandahar. He attended his brother's wedding and stayed at the party until 1:30 A.M. Later speaking of al-Qaeda, Karzai said, "They don't want peace and stability in Afghanistan. They want Afghanistan to be in conflict, they want Afghanistan to be in sorrow. But they should know that Afghanistan is united, and that Afghanistan will not be pressured by Al Qaeda and the terrorists."

The president's spirit is heartening, but recent events continue to be troubling. In March 2003, Taliban forces attacked a group of Red Cross workers in southern Afghanistan and killed the only foreign worker among them, a water engineer from El Salvador. He was the first foreign aid worker to die in Afghanistan since the Taliban's downfall 18 months earlier. The message the Taliban was sending was clear: Foreign workers who support the Karzai government are not safe.

While Taliban fighters continue to creep back into the country, warlords, especially in the north, are returning to their old ways of fighting one another for land and power. "It's like I am seeing the same movie twice and no one is trying to fix the problem," said Ahmed Wali Karzai, the president's brother and his representative in Kandahar. "What was promised to Afghans with the collapse of the Taliban was a new life of hope and change. But what was delivered? Nothing. Everyone is back in business."

Yet it is not too late to save Afghanistan if the international community fully commits itself to helping. An UN-sponsored three-year plan to disarm 100,000 Afghan militiamen, many of them in the private armies of warlords, begins in July 2003. The ultimate goal of the program is to reintegrate these fighters into civilian life and retrain them to find new jobs in a conflict-free Afghanistan.

On May 1, 2003, the United States declared the end of the major combat phase of the coalition occupation. Officials made this public announcement in large part to encourage other nations, particularly in Europe, to come in and support major reconstruction efforts with money, technology, and expertise. Whether the country is safe enough for such reconstruction remains to be seen.

What is clear is that the Afghan people cannot rebuild their country alone. It will take the effort of the world's nations to transform this land in perpetual transition into a healthy, peaceful, and prosperous nation.

NOTES

p. 25 " 'Participants . . . took positions along a road . . .' " Major General Oleg Sarin and Col. Lev Dvoretsky. *The Afghan Syndrome: The Soviet Union's Vietnam* (Novato, California: Presidio Press, 1993), p. 97.

p. 26 " 'His mission in life . . .' " *New York Times*, September 8, 2002, p. 23.

p. 30 "'Islamic faith is a bright light . . .'" *New York Times Magazine*, September 30, 2001, p. 49.

p. 31 "'Even if it [the United States] were twice as strong . . .'" "Mullah Omar—in his own words." Guardian Unlimited website. Available on-line. URL: http://www.guardian.co.uk/g2/story/o,3604,558076,00.html. Downloaded on November 25, 2002.

p. 33 "'The destruction by the Taliban . . .'" Jamey Keaton. "Memory of Small Statues Celebrated." Afghan Info Center website. Available on-line. URL: http://www.afghan-info.com/Research_Articles/Taliban_DestroyStatues.htm#memory. Downloaded on December 18, 2002.

p. 33 "'In October [1996] one woman . . .'" Michael Griffin. *Reaping the Whirlwind: The Taliban Movement in Afghanistan* (Sterling, Virginia: Pluto Press, 2001), p. 158.

pp. 33–34 "'Once I went shopping . . .'" Rosemarie Skaine. *The Women of Afghanistan Under the Taliban* (Jefferson, North Carolina: McFarland & Company, 2002), pp. 89–90.

p. 37 "'The Taliban were not from the masses . . .'" *New York Times Magazine*, September 30, 2001.

p. 38 "'Let us be good to each other . . .'" *New York Times*, December 23, 2001, p. A1.

p. 40 "They don't want peace and stability . . ." *New York Times*, September 7, 2002, p. A7.

p. 40 "'It's like I am seeing the same movie . . .'" *Connecticut Post*, April 8, 2003, p. A10.

PART II
Afghanistan Today

4

GOVERNMENT

Afghanistan has been ruled by a bewildering variety of governments since 1964, most of them authoritarian with little or no representation for the Afghan people. The kind of centralized, democratic government enjoyed in the United States and other Western countries has been elusive for Afghans. Whimsical warlords have often been the only stable rulers in a city or province. Those kings, presidents, and prime ministers who have fashioned a national government in Kabul have usually had a difficult if not impossible task of imposing their rule beyond the borders of the capital.

A Series of Governments

The modern era of government began in 1964, when King Zahir Shah called a *loya jirga* to approve and pass into law a new national constitution. The document was praised as the finest of its kind in the Muslim world up to that time, and all subsequent constitutions in Afghanistan have been based on it. It proclaimed the country a constitutional monarchy, a form of government where the power of the king or queen is limited by the laws of the constitution. This arrangement secures certain rights for the citizenry.

In 1973, the king was overthrown by his cousin, former prime minister Daoud Khan, who declared Afghanistan a republic. The title was deceptive, however, because Daoud Khan ruled the country as a benign dictator, allowing no other political parties to operate. In a military coup four years later, communists took over. Under them, all property and power belonged to the state. Their socialistic agenda was largely rejected by the people, and they remained in power only with the support of the Soviets, who then invaded the country in December 1979. After the Communist regime fell in 1992, feuding warlords quickly plunged the country back into civil war. From this chaos, emerged the Taliban who promised law and order but delivered as repressive a regime as Afghanistan had ever known.

With the fall of the Taliban in 2001, Afghanistan is ready to try again to become a democratic republic. This time, with real representation in all branches of government and the strong support of the United States and other Western nations, true democracy might work.

The President and Council of Ministers

Like the United States, the new Afghan government is headed by a president who holds executive powers that he uses to run the government and enact laws. President Hamid Karzai (see sidebar on p. 48) was appointed interim chairman of the government in December 2001 by the 30-member Afghanistan Interim Authority (AIA) meeting in Bonn, Germany. The following June he was overwhelmingly elected interim president of a transitional government by the *loya jirga,* or grand council (see sidebar). His term of office will end in June 2004 when a national election will be held to determine the next full-term government.

President Karzai has an eight-member Council of Ministers that is responsible, with him, for setting domestic and foreign policy. Three of the most powerful positions in this Council are held by Tajik leaders of the Northern Alliance, the group that fought side by side with U.S. forces to defeat the Taliban. The Tajiks, the second largest ethnic group, hold the balance of power in the government. The Pashtuns, the largest ethnic group, to which Karzai belongs, are underrepresented.

There are two women on the Council—Sima Samar, the Commissioner of Human Rights (see sidebar, chapter 10) and Dr. Sohaila Siddeqi, a leading Pashtun surgeon, and Minister of Public Health.

Unlike the American government, the Afghan government has four vice presidents. The only Pashtun vice president, Hajji Abdul Qadir, was assassinated in July 2002, creating an imbalance of power and representation in the government.

President Karzai has earned the respect and support of many Afghans for his courage and determination. His primary goals are to make the nation safe, to promote education and health care, and to improve the nation's roadways, many of which are impassable (see sidebar, chapter 10). He has the firm support of the United States and other Western nations, but he will also need the support of the political leaders who have traditionally complicated every Afghan leader's job—the warlords.

The Warlords—Afghanistan's Power Brokers

The provincial warlords have been a powerful force in Afghan politics for centuries. Their positions of leadership in the tribal clans have given them an authority on the local level that many of them have used to gather personal wealth and power. In this century, the warlords, together with the Islamic religious leaders, have often worked to thwart the establishment of a central government in Kabul. They have also fought each other, creating a dangerous atmosphere of war and lawlessness. Only when facing a common enemy, such as the Soviets or the Taliban, have the warlords forgotten their differences and worked together toward a common goal. With the Taliban gone, some warlords have gone back to their old ways, attacking a city or province to assert their power over another warlord. A few have even misled American forces into bombing their personal enemies, claiming that they were members of the Taliban or al-Qaeda.

Not all warlords are so ruthless and selfish. Tajik warlord Ismail Kahn, one of the ablest of the Northern Alliance commanders, kept order and peace in Herat province during the violent civil strife of the early 1990s. At the other end of the spectrum is the brutal Uzbek warlord Rashid Dostum, the former head of the secret police during the Communist years. Dostum's troops committed some of the worse atrocities against captured Taliban troops.

HAMID KARZAI (b. 1957)

A leader with a strong nationalist spirit and a largely secular outlook, Hamid Karzai may be just the kind of president Afghanistan needs to lead it into a new era.

He was born in Kandahar on December 24, 1957, into the Popolzai clan, one of the most powerful of the Pashtun groups. Mohammad Zahir Shah, the king at that time, is his cousin.

When the Soviets invaded Afghanistan, the Karzai family fled to Pakistan. Karzai, who earned a bachelor of arts (BA) degree at the Habibia School in Kabul, received his masters degree (MA) in political science from the Himachal Paradesh University in Simla, India. In 1983, he moved to the United States where he helped open Helmand, the first restaurant in a successful family chain. While there, he also raised funds for a mujahideen group who were fighting the Soviets in Afghanistan.

Hamid Karzai (center, front row) prays as he is sworn in as Afghanistan's interim prime minister in December 2001. Given the many problems his government will face in a country devastated by more than two decades of war, prayers seem very appropriate to the occasion. (AP/Wide World Photos/Marco Di Lauro)

Following the Soviet withdrawal, Karzai served as deputy foreign minister in the Rabbani government. When civil war tore the country apart in 1994, he resigned his post. Karzai was an early supporter of the Taliban who emerged from his hometown, but by 1997 he was disillusioned with their repressive reign and broke away from them. He risked his life traveling in the Taliban-held territory in the south to convince Pashtun warlords to fight against the Taliban. His father, Abdul Ahad Karzai, a former parliamentary deputy, was assassinated by the Taliban in 1999.

With his Western education (he speaks seven languages) and skill as a negotiator, Karzai is seen as a model leader by the Americans and has earned the support of many Afghans.

Today, as the country's legitimately elected president, Hamid Karzai is working to lead all Afghans into a new, better multiethnic society. "Our objective," he said after his election in June 2002, "is to bring the Afghan people dignity and the good life that they so very much deserve."

Today, Dostum has been brought into the Karzai government as a deputy defense minister and the vice president representing the north. Whether men like Dostum can shed their old ways and make amends for the past, is a key question. The answer could spell success or disaster for the new government.

Role of the King

Afghanistan's last king, Mohammad Zahir Shah, was deposed more than 30 years ago, and there is little chance this land will ever again become a monarchy. However, the 87-year-old Zahir Shah returned from exile in April 2002, to receive a hero's welcome from the Afghan people. Many of them see him as a central figure in their country's future.

They consider King Zahir's 30-year reign as the last time Afghanistan knew peace and stability. Although not a dynamic leader, he was a well-meaning monarch, in sharp contrast to most of the rulers who followed

This Afghan photo shop owner living in Pakistan proudly displays a portrait of formerly exiled king Zahir Shah, seen by many Afghans as the one man who can unite a divided and broken people. (AP/Wide World Photos/ B. K. Bangash)

him. For this, and his important role in fashioning the first successful Afghan constitution, Zahir continues to be revered by many of his fellow Pashtuns. He is also seen as a symbol of the nationalist spirit, a father figure who alone can bring together the diverse ethnic groups that make up the population.

Before his arrival in Afghanistan, the Tajiks were fearful the King would serve as a rallying point for the Pashtun majority and threaten their own power. Since then, however, they have come to accept Zahir's role as a peacemaker and conciliator. It was powerful and fitting that he should convene the *loya jirga* in June 2002 that elected his kinsman, Hamid Karzai, as president.

As Obaidullah Buhil Abid, a middle-aged politician, said of the former king, "Today, I think, he is the only man who can unite this nation."

THE *LOYA JIRGA*—AFGHANISTAN'S MOST POWERFUL LEGISLATIVE BODY

While the Meli Shura, the National Assembly, is the designated legislative body in the new government, it is not the most powerful one. For more than two centuries, the *loya jirga*, or grand council, has been the primary arbitrator of power in the country.

The *loya jirga* brings together all the leaders of the land, including provincial warlords, national delegates, and government officials, all of whom are selected by their local leadership. Together they make momentous decisions that affect the entire country. Kings and presidents have called *loya jerga* to decide a successor to a king, authorize a coup, or make a major reform law.

Perhaps the most important *loya jirga* in modern times was the one called by King Zahir Shah in 1964 that drew up a ground-breaking national constitution. The constitution made the *loya jirga* itself an integral part of government policy, no longer the tool of the current party in power.

Not all *loya jerga* have achieved their intended goals. In 1928 King Amanullah called for a council to push through a program of reform and modernization, but it was rejected by the 1,000 delegates. He then called a smaller *jirga* of 100 handpicked loyalists, which passed his program without contesting it. The people, however, rejected the reforms and Amanullah was ousted from power within a year. Today, as then, the *loya jirga* remains the voice of the Afghan people.

The National Assembly

Afghanistan has not had a functioning legislative body since civil war erupted in June 1993. The National Assembly, first founded in 1964, is the highest, permanent legislative body in the country and was reformed in June 2002 by the *loya jirga*. It is comprised of two houses, or councils. The Council of Elders has 192 members, some of whom are elected and others appointed by the president. The Council of Representatives has 234 members, all of whom are elected. The National Assembly makes laws with the approval of the president and the Council of Ministers, just as the U.S. Congress does.

The Judiciary

Tribal codes and laws regulated justice in Afghanistan until the 20th century. A judicial system existed under the kings after Habibullah, but was largely defunct by the 1990s. The Bonn Agreement called for the formation of a judicial commission to construct a new Western-style justice system that would also include Islamic principles. There is an already functioning Afghan Supreme Court whose members have been appointed by the president. Lower courts are also in place in most of the country's 32 provinces. They handle civil and criminal cases.

Political Parties

As of early 2003, there were no political parties of national prominence in Afghanistan. There are several reasons for this. First, political power has traditionally resided with powerful warlords and monarchs who have been supported by ethnic groups. Secondly, there is nothing in the current Afghan constitution, created in 1964, that addresses the issue of political parties and how they should be formed. Without legal protection, many political organizers are reluctant to form parties. Finally, economic conditions are so terrible in post-Taliban Afghanistan that most people are just trying to get by and have little time or energy to pursue politics.

The few political parties that do exist are typically ethnically and religiously based such as the Jamiat-i-Islami, an Islamic party made up of mostly Tajiks, or the Hezb-i-Wahdat, a party of Shi'ite Muslim groups who are mostly Hazaras. An exception is the Nehzat-i-Melli, or National Party, formed in 2002 by education minister and internal security adviser Mohammad Yunis Qanuni. Qanuni has declared his party open to all ethnic groups, and it is possible he will use the party as a launching pad for a presidential bid in 2004 when the first full-term national elections are held.

Local Government

Afghanistan is divided into 32 provinces. They are Badakhshan, Badghis, Baghlan, Balkh, Bamian, Farah, Faryab, Ghazni, Ghowr, Helmand, Herat, Jowzjan, Kabol, Kandahar, Kapisa, Khowst, Konar, Kondoz, Laghman, Lowgar, Nangarhar, Nimruz, Nurestan, Oruzgan, Paktia, Paktika, Parvan, Samangan, Sar-e Pol, Takhar, Vardak, and Zabol.

Each province is administered by a governor appointed by the central government in Kabul. In reality, control of a number of provinces still lies in the hands of local warlords and chiefs. Provinces are further divided into districts and subdistricts.

The Armed Forces

Civil war and the Taliban regime left Afghanistan without a standing army. The sole homegrown military presence since the Taliban's fall has been the armies of the Northern Alliance, a coalition formed by warlords and other leaders of the resistance. Today, as commander in chief of the armed services, President Karzai is working with international help to form a national army. Officers are being trained at the recently reopened military school in Kabul. Afghanistan also has a small air force with bases at Jalalabad and two smaller cities.

International Peacekeepers

The main military presence in Afghanistan today is the 5,500-strong international peacekeeping force, officially known as the International Security Assistance Force (ISAF). It was created by the United Nations in December 2001. These soldiers hail from 22 different countries, though most come from Great Britain, Germany, and the Netherlands. Among the other countries participating are Spain, Turkey, and the Czech Republic.

The peacekeepers' purpose is to keep order in Kabul and help bolster the new government of Hamid Karzai. While most of the additional 8,000 American troops stationed in the country are out in the countryside, hunting down al-Qaeda and the remaining Taliban, the ISAF has limited its activities to the capital, where they patrol the streets 24 hours a day in armored cars, jeeps, and tanks. President Karzai has praised the peacekeepers' efforts and urged their countries to supply more soldiers to patrol other parts of the country. So far they have been reluctant to do so. One reason is the danger facing the peacekeepers from al-Qaeda operatives and their sympathizers. As of February 2003, 14 peacekeepers have been killed on duty, including seven German soldiers who perished in a helicopter crash in Kabul on December 21, 2002. In early February 2003, Germany and the Netherlands took over command of the ISAF from Turkey.

NOTES

p. 49 "'Our objective is to bring . . .'" *New York Times*, June 15, 2002, p. A4.

p. 50 "'Today, I think, he is the only man . . .'" *New York Times*, April 19, 2002, p. A15.

5

RELIGION

Religion, specifically Islam, has been the glue that has held together the various ethnic groups and tribes in Afghanistan and given them a common destiny. It kept them strong and defiant through the 10-year war against antireligious Communists, both at home and in the Soviet Union. But religion has also contributed to Afghanistan's many problems. For more than a century, reactionary Islamic leaders joined forces with Afghan warlords to block the road to much-needed modernization in every area of Afghan life.

More recently, the fanatical fundamentalists of the Taliban further twisted religion, taking it to an intolerable extreme that oppressed an entire society. Even with the downfall of the Taliban, serious questions remain as to what role religion should play in the future of this religious country.

An Islamic Nation

Islam is the major religion of Afghanistan. Some 99 percent of Afghans are Muslims, followers of Islam. This great monotheistic faith first came to Afghanistan in the seventh century and it has been the dominant religion ever since.

Muslim in Arabic means "one who submits to God" and the Muslims do so by meeting certain obligations, which include praying five times a day to Allah (God), giving a portion of their income to the poor and needy, fasting during the holy month of Ramadan, and making a pilgrimage, if possible, to the holy city of Mecca. Mecca, in Saudi Arabia, is the hometown of Islam's founder and leading prophet, Muhammad.

There are two main sects of Islam: Sunni Muslims and Shi'ite Muslims. The Sunnis are descendants of the followers of Muhammad who follow the practices of the Sunna, or the prophet's example. They believed that Muhammad's successors should be drawn from among his companions. The Shi'ites supported the leadership of Muhammad's son-in-law and cousin, Ali. After Ali's death, they agreed to support only those Islamic leaders descended from Muhammad's family.

Over the centuries the two sects developed their own traditions and rules. About 84 percent of all Afghan Muslims are Sunni. Some 15 percent are Shi'ite, and most of them belong to three ethnic groups—the Hazaras, Kezilbal, and Isma'ilis.

Mosques, Mullahs, Muezzins, and Minarets

Both Sunni and Shi'ites meet to pray in mosques, Muslim houses of worship. The word mosque is derived from the Arabic word *marjid*, "a place of kneel-

Afghan Muslims pray inside Mazar-i-Sharif's Blue Mosque. The word mosque is derived from an Arabic word meaning "a place of kneeling." (AP/Wide World Photos/Efrem Lukatsky)

ing." Muslims usually pray in a kneeling position, which explains why there are no seats or pews in mosques. The holy day for worship for Muslims is Friday. At noon on Fridays, a crier, or muezzin, calls them to worship from a tall narrow tower called a minaret. Most mosques have from one to six minarets. When the worshippers enter the mosque, they wash their face, hands, and feet in a fountain located in a court area. Then the men form rows, with the women lining up behind them. A religious leader called a mullah (Islam has no priests) delivers a sermon after which the praying begins. The prayers are led by a chief officer in the mosque called the imam. He faces Mecca and the men and women follow his lead, bowing and kneeling as they recite passages from the Qur'an, the holy book of Islam.

THE ROLE OF THE MULLAH

While the mullah is not a priest or rabbi in the Christian or Jewish sense, his role in Afghan society is probably more influential than either of these religious figures.

Young men seeking to become mullahs study at a religious college called a *madrasa*. Here they study the Qur'an and Islam's many religious codes and laws. When they graduate, they can work as religious teachers in *madrasas* or other schools or serve as an official in a mosque, speaking to the faithful and performing other duties.

The most important mullahs in large city mosques are appointed by the government with the approval of the community. Besides speaking, they officiate at such important rituals as births, marriages, and deaths. They are highly respected members of the community and serve as arbitrators in disputes about religious interpretation. They also hold strong positions of authority in all matters religious and social.

Not all mullahs, however, are so respected. In rural areas, many mullahs are part-timers, earning their living as farmers or craftspersons. Some of them are barely more educated than their neighbors, and their opinions are often looked on suspiciously or even ignored. Some village mullahs are even seen as troublesome busybodies.

The mullahs' power, even in the cities, was recently undercut by the new government attempting to secularize laws and mores. The mullahs, however, continue to be a power to reckon with in Afghan society and will probably remain so for a long time to come.

Hindus and Sikhs

Of the one percent of Afghans who are not Muslims, most are Hindus, Sikhs, and Jews. Hinduism is one of the world's oldest religions and originated in India. The religion was largely driven out of Afghanistan along with Buddhism when the Muslims took over the country. Sikhism is a much newer religion. It was founded in the early 16th century as a blending of Hinduism and Islam. While Hindus are polytheistic, worshiping many gods, Sikhs, like Muslims, believe in one god.

Up until the early 1990s, there were about 50,000 Sikhs and Hindus in Afghanistan who lived together peacefully with their Muslim neighbors. When militant Hindus attacked a mosque in northern India in the early 1990s, Hindus and Sikhs in Afghanistan were endangered. Several Hindu temples were burned and looted in 1992 and 1993.

When the Taliban took power in 1996, they persecuted Sikhs and Hindus. They banned music and dancing at Sikh religious ceremonies, forced Sikhs and Hindu to display yellow cloths outside their homes, and ordered them to wear yellow tags on their persons to identify them. When the Taliban fell, thousands of Hindus and Sikhs were free to leave the country and settle in other parts of Asia, Great Britain, and the United States. Today only about 2,000 Hindus and Sikhs remain in Afghanistan. In December 2001, the Sikhs were promised their own office in the Bureau of Islamic Affairs.

The Jews of Afghanistan

Jews have lived in Afghanistan since the late 12th century when Jewish traders from Iran settled in Herat in western Afghanistan. Long a tolerated minority, Afghan Jews began immigrating to the new state of Israel in the Middle East after it was formed in 1948. Other Jews moved to Great Britain and the United States. Most of the remaining Jews left during the civil war that followed the Soviet-Afghan War. By the time the Taliban took power, only five Jewish families remained in Kabul. By 2002, only two middle-aged men remained. Ironically, they did not get along with each other and quarreled for control of the one synagogue still operating in Kabul. The men, however, have stayed faithful to their religion, even when arrested by the Taliban in 1998. "I told them, 'I am Jewish,'" recalled Isaak Levie, one of the two men. "If you slice me into pieces, I will not convert."

It is that spirit that has kept the Jewish faith alive, despite its low numbers, in this Islamic nation.

Other Religions

Buddhism was introduced in Afghanistan as early as 537 B.C., when two brothers, Tapassu and Bhallika, merchants of Bactria, took Buddhist vows. Bhallika later became a monk and built a Buddhist monastery near present-day Mazar-i-Sharif.

Buddhism flourished in eastern Afghanistan during the reign of Kanishka, the Kushan ruler in the first and second centuries A.D. Between the third and fifth centuries, Buddhists built two huge statues of Buddha, the largest of their kind in the world, in the Bamiyon Valley of the Hindu Kush Mountains. They hewed the statues out of sand rock and used a mixture of mud and straw to create the faces, hands, and the folds of the robes. These spectacular works of art and faith were destroyed by the Taliban in 2001 (see chapter 7).

The rise of Islam in the seventh century weakened Buddhism, but it continued to have its followers. In the early 14th century, the religion completely died out in Afghanistan.

Before Buddhism and Islam, there was another religion that many Afghans followed. Zoroastrianism was founded by the Persian prophet Zoroaster (also known as Zarathustra) sometime in the late seventh century B.C. (see sidebar). The religion, which sees life as a constant struggle between good and evil, later flourished in Persia. Only about 10,000 people follow Zoroastrianism today mostly in Iran and India. Only a very few of these followers of Zoroaster live in Afghanistan.

Older than Zoroastrianism are the pagan religions of ancient Afghanistan that still survive in some of the superstitions of rural Afghans. These simple, uneducated people fear evil spirits and wear amulets and other charms to protect themselves from their influence.

ZOROASTER (ca. 628–ca. 551 B.C.)

Zoroaster founded one of the world's oldest religions. He was not from Afghanistan, but found his first converts there. Little is known about his life except that he was most likely born in northwestern Persia. In Persian, his name is Zarathustra, which means "camel handler." At age 20, he left home and began a 10-year sojourn in search of religious truth. At 30, he experienced the first of seven revelations given to him by God (who he called Ahura Mazda) and his angels. Zoroastrianism, the religion he founded, sees life as a constant battle between good, represented by Ahura Mazda, and evil, represented by his enemy, Angra Mainyer. At the time of death, each person is judged by Ahura Mazda by which side he or she fought on. All history, according to Zoroastrianism, is divided into four eras, the last era being when Ahura Mazda reveals himself on Earth and oversees the final judgment of all souls, living and dead.

Zoroaster initially met with little success in his homeland of Persia. He traveled to Chorasmia, now part of present-day Afghanistan, where the Chorasmian king, Vishtaspa, converted to Zoroastrianism. The new religion quickly spread throughout

Although he was Persian, Zoroaster, founder of Zoroastrianism, gained his first converts in ancient Afghanistan, where, according to legend, he also died around 551 B.C. (Courtesy Free Library of Philadelphia)

his kingdom. According to legend, Zoroaster, was killed in Afghanistan about 551 B.C. By that time his religion was beginning to be accepted in his native Persia.

Zoroastrianism was suppressed by Alexander the Great when he conquered Persia in the 330s B.C. It experienced a revival about 400 years later, but was banned again by the Muslims when they came to power in Central Asia.

Few people practice this ancient religion today, but Zoroastrianism has had a strong influence on Judaism, Christianity, and Islam.

Religion Today

In his inauguration speech in late 2001, Hamid Karzai promised to grant freedom of worship to the followers of all religions under his interim government. But there are still conservative Muslims in Afghanistan who do not want to accept other religions. Fundamentalist religious and political leaders are also suspicious of returning Afghan exiles, many of them educated in the West. While not as extreme in their thinking as the Taliban, these conservative clerics and their followers see secularization and modernization as threats to traditional Afghan society. Inside and outside of the new government, people have many strong opinions about how Islam should shape the nation's future.

Mirjan Sarawaq, a young military commander, perhaps speaks for the majority of Afghans when he says "Religion should be separate from government. But we want a government based on Islamic principles."

NOTES
p. 59 "'I told them I am Jewish . . .'" *New York Times*, January 18, 2002, p. A4.
p. 61 "'Religion should be separate . . .'" Raghavan, Sudarsan, and Jonathan S. Landay. "Religion in Afghanistan: New rulers welcome non-Muslims." Freep.com. Available on-line. URL: http://www.freep.com./news/nw/islam24_20011224.htm. Downloaded on October 24, 2002.

6

THE ECONOMY

Twenty-two years of war and chaos have taken their toll on the Afghan economy. Before the Soviet invasion of 1979, there was some hope that a modern market economy, based on free enterprise, would take hold there. Economic growth had been stimulated by financial and technical aid from the United States and the Soviet Union in the mid-1950s. Industry, while still in its infancy, was starting to play a larger role in the economy. Irrigation projects increased agricultural production and created a profitable surplus that could be exported.

The Soviet-Afghan War, and the civil strife that followed it, wiped out this promise. Today, the Afghan economy is again in a shambles, and Afghanistan remains one of the world's poorest countries. The gross domestic product (GDP) per capita was only $700 in 2002. In Iran, another Muslim country, it was $7,000 the same year. With the democratic, central government established in 2002, comes the hope that a stable economy can be built. Few people have illusions that it will be easy.

Agriculture

For centuries, Afghanistan's economy has been almost entirely based on agriculture. Seven out of ten workers are farmers, agricultural workers, or herders, while the remaining 30 percent of the work force is in industry and services. While agriculture dominates the economy, the country's annual harvest is meager at best. Only a little more than a tenth of the land is arable, and much of that must be irrigated heavily to produce crops.

Irrigation projects came to a sudden halt when the Soviets invaded, and they remain unfinished today. As a result, arable land is limited. Agricultural production remains at a subsistence level for millions of small farmers, and the problem is compounded by an almost complete lack of new technology in farming methods. To furrow their land, Afghan farmers still use wooden plows pulled by oxen. They have little fertilizer, and they plant seeds of poor quality. Additionally, even where the government has attempted to introduce new, more productive techniques, the majority of farmers have rejected them, preferring to cling to the old ways.

Afghanistan's chief crops are wheat and other grains, such as barley, corn, and rice. Sugar beets, sugarcane, and cotton are also important crops. Most of the production comes from the north, where the soil is most fertile. Fruit orchards in the valleys of Kabul and Arghandab yield apples, pears, peaches, apricots, plums, and cherries. Fertile vineyards in Herat and Kandahar produce more than 30 varieties of grapes and some excellent wines. Nut trees yield great amounts of almonds, walnuts, pine nuts, and pistachios. Dried fruits and nuts are exported to neighboring Pakistan and India.

Raising livestock is also important to the Afghan economy. Sheep are Afghanistan's most highly prized domestic animals. The country's Karakul sheep are world-famous for their warm wool and beautiful pelts. Most Persian lamb coats in the United States are made of Karakul wool. One and a half million cattle produce dairy products and beef, and about seven million chickens provide poultry. Cow milk accounts for about two-thirds of the nation's milk production; the remaining third comes from the country's two million goats and more than 14 million sheep. Horses, donkeys, and camels are used primarily for transportation.

Opium and Heroin

Afghanistan's most profitable agricultural product is not one that most Afghans are proud of. In 1999, 2000, and 2002, Afghanistan had the dubious honor of being the world's number-one producer of raw opium. Opium poppies, grown in the northeastern mountains along the Pakistani border in the remote provinces of Nangarhar, Badahksha, Helmond, and Pakita, are transported to laboratories in Nangarhar and Pakistan. They are refined into opium and heroin and then exported to India, Iran, Europe, and the United States. Some farmers also grow marijuana.

Despite continuing pressure from the United States, Afghanistan's attempts to end the opium trade have been largely unsuccessful. The temptation to dabble in illegal trade is too great, especially for Afghanistan's desperately poor farmers. Profits from opium and heroin financed the mujahideen's fight against the Soviets and the Communist regime in the 1980s, and their fight against the Taliban in the late 1990s. Efforts being made to end the drug trade will be discussed in the last chapter of this book.

Natural Resources—Untapped Treasures

If the Afghan economy is to grow in the future, much depends on the development of its natural resources. While most of the country's forests have been cut down over centuries, Afghanistan is rich in minerals. The main challenge to exploiting these minerals is logistical and technological—getting to where the minerals are, extracting them from the earth, and then transporting them to local and foreign markets.

Great deposits of high-grade iron ore north of Kabul remain untouched because Afghanistan lacks the resources to mine it. Copper has been mined and refined on a small scale at a processing plant near Kabul. Some uranium has been extracted in mountains east of the capital. They are also largely untapped deposits of zinc, lead, mica, gold, silver, nickel, salt, beryllium, and chrome ore.

Afghanistan has had greater success in producing precious and semiprecious gemstones, including amethyst, rubies, topaz, kunzite, and tourmaline. The most sought-after gemstone is lapis lazuli (see sidebar).

Afghanistan's most exploited natural resource, and its largest export, is natural gas. Natural gas deposits were first discovered in 1967 by the Soviets at Khwaja Gogurdak. For years, most of the gas was sold to the Soviet Union to pay for Soviet imports. After the breakup of the Soviet

THE BLUE BEAUTY—LAPIS LAZULI

Lapis lazuli literally means "blue stone," and no other gem is so rich in that color. The mines of Afghanistan's Kokcha River valley in the northern province of Badakhshan produce more of this semiprecious stone than any other place on earth.

The mined stone is sent to a lapidarium in Kabul, where it is cut and polished for sale. Because of its beauty, lapis lazuli is displayed simply, without elaborate settings.

The ancient Egyptians and Romans prized the blue stone both as a bodily ornament and as a medicine. They ground it into a fine powder, mixed it with milk, and used the mixture to dress boils and skin ulcers. The stone was also ground into a pigment, natural ultramarine, used for painting. Today an artificially made pigment provides ultramarine.

Union in 1991, natural gas continued to be sent to Russia to pay off Afghanistan's large debt to that country.

Accessing Afghanistan's vast oil resources has not been as successful. Although the United States helped discover oil as far back as 1936, neither they nor any other Western nation has committed to developing the Afghan oil industry.

Afghanistan's best hope for cheap oil might be in neighboring Turkmenistan to the northwest, which, although landlocked, has extensive oil and natural gas fields. The United States has proposed running a pipeline through Afghanistan and Pakistan to get the oil and gas to the Arabian Sea, where it can be transported abroad.

American oil executives, however, are uneasy about local Afghan warlords who could stop the fuel as it passes over their lands and demand more money for the use of their territory. Executives also fear that the warlords will keep the transit fees for themselves and not give the local people their share. "So a pipeline, which could bring more cash into Afghanistan than any other step short of legalizing opium, could just as easily promote destabilization and upheaval," wrote *New York Times* reporter Stephen Kinzer. Until the central government in Kabul can control the warlords, the $2 billion pipeline is unlikely to become a reality.

Manufacturing and Industry

While many countries in Europe experienced industrial revolutions in the early 18th and 19th centuries, modern industry did not come to Afghanistan until the 1920s. The government helped start small factories to manufacture shoes, ceramics, soap, and other consumer products. Tanneries and cotton-ginning mills were also established. Cement factories were started with aid from the Soviet Union in the mid-1950s. But industry has made little progress since the 1970s. Cotton and wool mills remain among the largest industries, followed by factories that produce such consumer products as rayon, furniture, and construction materials. A thriving fertilizer plant in Mazar-i-Sharif is powered by natural gas.

Far more important to the Afghan economy are the cottage industries of skilled craftspeople who work out of their homes or in small shops.

Handicrafts made by skilled craftspersons and light manufacturing still forms a far more substantial part of the Afghan economy than heavy industry. Here, a shop owner exhibits many different Afghan caps for his customers. (Courtesy Library of Congress)

THE BAZAAR—AFGHANISTAN'S BUSIEST MARKETPLACE

In the United States, a bazaar is a one-time sale of various items for a charity. In Afghanistan and many Asian countries, a bazaar is the equivalent of a shopping mall, but far more colorful and exciting.

An Afghan bazaar is a market place that can encompass one narrow street or a whole section of a town or city. The Great Bazaar in Kabul was immense. It was considered one of the wonders of Asia until British soldiers destroyed it during the First Anglo-Afghan War in 1842.

Traders, merchants, and craftspeople sell a bewildering array of food and goods in tiny stalls and shops, some of them only a few feet wide. While much of the merchandise is made locally, many of the items for sale are imported from a multitude of countries. On a visit to the Ishkamish bazaar during the 1980s one foreign correspondent was amazed to find "Turkish cooking oil with vitamins added, Moon Rabbi underwear from North Korea, an orange drink from Holland, small oil

The bazaar has been a mainstay of Afghanistan's local economy for centuries. This picture shows the main street of the Great Bazaar of Kabul in 1842, shortly before it was destroyed by the British in the First Anglo-Afghan War. (Courtesy Library of Congress)

(continues)

(continued)

lamps from Germany, and three kinds of strong, heat-resistant glasses from France, used for drinking tea."

Buying and bartering are not the only activities that take place in the bazaar. It is a central meeting place, where family and friends can get together to exchange the latest news and gossip. For Afghans of all ages, the bazaar is a shopping mall, a meeting place, and a news center.

These include leather workers, metalsmiths, coppersmiths, jewelry makers, potters, basket weavers, and carpet makers. The most prized of Afghan homemade products are its carpets and rugs which are valued for their meticulous craftsmanship and intricate designs and exported abroad in great numbers. Nearly as popular are the warm, handsome sheepskin coats made in Ghazni.

Tourism

While industry remains underdeveloped in Afghanistan today, tourism is nearly nonexistent. The last tourist boom was in the early 1990s, immediately after the withdrawal of the Soviets and prior to the outbreak of civil war. In 1990, 8,000 tourists came to the country. The number dropped drastically during the years of the Taliban and terrorists. The most recent figures from 1998 show the tourist industry generating about $1 million.

Now that peace has returned to the country, what does Afghanistan have that would attract foreign tourists? Surprisingly, a lot. Few central Asian countries have as rich a history and as many historic sites going back to ancient times. Combine this with the natural beauty of Afghanistan's mountains and valleys and it has tremendous potential as a tourist destination.

But in order to attract tourists, the government needs to develop the infrastructure to accommodate them. This means reliable airline service, better hotels, and other facilities tourists require. To make this happen, the central government needs to bring stability to the country and make it secure and safe for foreign visitors.

Foreign Trade

Through the 1980s, Afghanistan's principal trading partner was the Soviet Union. Today, more than a decade after the breakup of the Soviet Union, Russia is just one of the countries Afghanistan does business with. Major trading partners include such neighboring countries as Pakistan, India, and Saudi Arabia, as well as such Western nations as Great Britain, the Czech Republic, and Germany. Since the U.S. military arrived in 2001, the United States has begun a trading program with Afghanistan. What role it will take in the future of the country's trade and economy remains to be seen.

Afghanistan's exports in 1996, the last year statistics are available, totaled an estimated $80 million, excluding the illegal drug trade. Leading exports include natural gas, cotton, fruit, nuts, sheepskins, rugs, and wool. Afghanistan's imports in 1996 were an estimated $150 million. Leading imports include such industrially-made products as machinery, textiles, motor vehicles, and petroleum products, as well as wheat, sugar, processed animal and vegetable oils, and tea.

Foreign Aid

During the Cold War, foreign aid flooded into Afghanistan from the Soviet Union and the United States. That aid slowed down to a trickle during the rule of the Taliban. Now more than 60 countries and international financial organizations want to help Afghanistan rebuilt. All of them made pledges totaling $4.5 billion through the year 2006 at the Tokyo Donors Conference for Afghanistan in January 2002. Yet, according to the World Bank and UN Development Program, this is less than a third of the $15 billion Afghanistan will need over the next decade to get back on its feet.

Critics claim much of this foreign aid will only bind Afghanistan more closely to the West and could actually slow down real national growth. Others argue that less money should be spent on emergency aid to people and more on the reconstruction of the country's infrastructure.

Banking and the Currency System

The largest bank in Afghanistan is the Central Bank, founded in 1938. It issues all banknotes, executes government loans, and loans money to other banks. Most money-lending and foreign exchange transactions are not performed by banks but "money bazaars" located in cities and towns.

One problem that has plagued Afghanistan's economy for decades is an unstable currency system. The unit of money, the afghani, has suffered tremendous inflation during years of war and instability. Prior to 1996, the official exchange rate was fixed by the Afghan government at 50.6 afgahanis to the U.S. dollar. In 1996, the free market exchange shot up to 2,262.65 afghanis to the dollar. Since then the exchange rate has continued to climb, reaching a high of 17,000 afghanis per dollar in December 1996. In January 2000, the rate was 4,750 to the dollar. People have had to carry huge bags of afghanis in order to make even the simplest of purchases. Further confusing the issue, are the currencies in the marketplace, including the Pakistani rupee, the U.S. dollar, and non-government afghanis produced by local warlords in the countryside, some of whom make money on their own printing presses.

To stabilize the currency and weaken the warlords' power, the government created a new afghani in 2002, which is worth 1,000 of the old afghanis. Through early December 2002, people could exchange their old currency for new bills. The government then burned the old money.

"We printed this money to rescue people from having to use different currencies," said President Karzai. "From now on, we'll have just one currency that everyone can use."

Now it is up to the government to develop new ways to stimulate the economy, provide new jobs, and improve the standard of living so people will have something to spend their money on.

Transportation

The lack of good transportation has been a serious stumbling block to improving the Afghan economy. There are only 16 miles of railroads in the entire country and few rivers that are navigable. Roadways are the major means of getting goods and people from place to place, and after 22 years of war and chaos they are in terrible condition. Nearly 3,000 miles of asphalt road have been destroyed since the Soviet invasion of 1979. Of the 13,000 miles of highways and roads remaining, many are impassable. This is bad news for the nation's 35,000 cars.

The best highways link Kabul with most of the other major cities, but do not penetrate the countryside beyond. Without a better road system, it is virtually impossible for the 32,000 commercial vehicles to get goods quickly to many parts of the country. A major priority of the Karzai government is to rebuild poor roads with financial aid from abroad.

Afghanistan had an estimated 45 airports in 2000, ten of them with paved runways. There are two international airports at Kabul and Kandahar. Most of the 35 smaller airports with unpaved runways serve provincial cities and towns and operate seasonally.

NOTES

p. 65 "'So a pipeline, which could bring . . .'" New York Times, March 17, 2002, Week in Review, p. 6.

pp. 67–68 "'Turkish cooking oil with vitamins added . . .'" Arthur Bonner, *Among the Afghans* (Durham, North Carolina: Duke University Press, 1987), p. 207.

p. 70 "'We printed the money to rescue people . . .'" *Connecticut Post*, October 8, 2002, p. C5.

7

CULTURE

When Afghanistan's National Gallery in Kabul reopened in March 2002, its exhibit featured broken picture frames and torn drawings. The unusual display was a grim reminder of how the Taliban's repressive regime weakened the national spirit of Afghanistan by destroying Afghan art and culture. Some 2,000 treasures were defaced or destroyed. The Taliban had interpreted Islamic law in a twisted and erroneous way as forbidding all figurative art. One courageous artist, Dr. Yousef Asefi, saved many paintings by covering the canvases over with watercolors, which he removed after the Taliban's fall from power.

"Our future depends on these [artists]," declared President Hamid Karzai at the gallery's reopening ceremony. "We need to save our culture and bring it forward, make a new culture of Afghanistan. This is at the top of our agenda."

His words have resonated with those who seek to build their country into a modern nation. In the past, Afghan culture has often been as fragile as the national spirit. Isolation from the outside world, constant warfare, and a tribal society that has not promoted education or individual expression, have all had a negative effect on Afghan culture.

The last great flowering of the arts took place in the 15th century under the Timurid dynasty. Yet despite centuries of neglect, the Afghans have clung to what culture they have and have refused to let it die.

Language

If a single, national language is the unifying factor in any culture, Afghanistan has sadly been lacking it. There are about as many languages spoken in the country as there are ethnic groups. Each language is further broken down into a number of dialects with their own distinct pronunciations and specialized vocabulary. The most-widely spoken language is Pashtu, the language of the Pashtuns, the largest ethnic group in Afghanistan. In 1936, in an effort to unite the diverse peoples of his country, King Zahir Shah established Pashtu as the official language. Since then Dari, also called Afghan Farsi, a language spoken by the Tajiks and closely related to Persian, has become the second official language. Many of Afghan's greatest writers have written in Dari, and it is the most spoken language of the nation's business community. Today, most Afghans can speak at least one of these two languages.

Among the other common languages in Afghanistan are an archaic Persian spoken by Hazaras, and a Turkic language spoken by Uzbeks, Turkmen, and the Kyrgyz people. The most popular foreign languages taught in Afghan schools are English, French, German, Italian, and Russian.

Literature

The dominating literacy form in Afghan literature from its beginnings has been poetry. In a land where the majority of adults are illiterate, there is a strong oral tradition. Poets and storytellers recite their work in village after village, passing it down from generation to generation. Each ethnic group has its own epic poems, songs, and historical sagas that have given its people a sense of historical and cultural identity and pride. One of the most celebrated epic poems is *Shah nameh* (Book of kings) written by the 11th century Persian poet Firdawsi. It is composed of 60,000 rhyming couplets in Dari.

The two most important Pashtu poets are the 17th century authors Kushal Khan Khattak (see sidebar on p. 74), widely regarded as the national poet of Afghanistan, and Abdur Rashman.

A prose tradition is derived largely from Persian literature, with its rich storehouse of love tales and children's animal fables. Folktales are appreciated by both children and adults and often are used to teach moral lessons and traditional values. Most contemporary Afghanistan novelists and short story writers write in Dari. The oral tradition was revived during the years of the Taliban regime. Contemporary poets such as Shir Mohammed Khara memorized their poems to avoid being caught by the Taliban religious police. They shared their work in underground meetings with other writers.

KUSHAL KHAN KHATTAK (1613–1690)

It is indicative of Afghan culture that its most revered writer is as admired for his military deeds as he is for his poetry. Kushal Khan Khattak was born near Peshawar in present-day Pakistan, and was the son of a tribal chief of the Khattak tribe.

He succeeded his father in 1641 at a time when Afghanistan was part of the Moghul Empire. When the new Moghul emperor Aurangzab came to power, he imprisoned Khattak in a fortress in Delhi. On his release, Khattak urged Pashtuns to rebel against the Moghuls and led local rebels into battle, earning him the title "Warrior Poet." He also wrote works on philosophy and medicine as well as an autobiography.

While his poetry often glorified the Afghan past to inspire his own tribe and others to unite against a common enemy, he was also surprisingly realistic about the vagaries of his countrymen. This comes through in this excerpt from one of his poems:

> Good men are like garnets and rubies,
> Not often to be found,
> While other common, worthless men,
> Like common stones, abound.

The appeal of Khattak's poetry was not limited to Afghanistan. When a British officer published a translation of his work in the late 19th century, it became a best seller in Great Britain.

Khattak's poetry remains vital in Afghanistan today. When rebel forces entered battle against the Soviets in the 1980s, many were reciting not the verses of the sacred Qur'an but the poetry of Kushal Khan Khattak.

Some writers live abroad in self-imposed exile. In 1988, the post Rariq Fani migrated to San Diego, California, with his family to escape the turmoil in Afghanistan. He continues however, to write passionately about his homeland.

Today, Afghan literature is promoted by two monthly periodicals. *Aryana*, published by the Afghan Historical Society, contains works relating to Afghan history. *Kabul* is published by the Pashtu Society, and is devoted to works of Pashtu literature, especially for non-Pashtu-reading Afghans.

Music

The Taliban repressed music just as severely as they repressed art and literature. They considered music a sin against Allah. Traditional Afghan musical instruments such as the six-stringed *rohab*; the *santur*, a type of zither; and the *chang*, a plucked mouth harp, were outlawed. Musicians had to hide them from Taliban police. A man could even be arrested for clapping his hands and a woman for humming to her baby.

"We lost so much," said Aziz Ghazmir, one of the country's top popular singers. "After five years of not singing at all, I was afraid to hear my own voice, and it was a very scary moment, to sing again for the first time."

Folk songs and folk dancing, the most vital and traditional of Afghan music, have returned to prominence since the fall of the Taliban. Afghan folk groups are accompanied by traditional wind and string instruments and drums beaten with the palms and fingers. Group dancing is earthy and celebratory and is part of any Afghan wedding or feast day. The national dance, the *attan* is, not surprisingly, a war dance that reenacts the life of ancient Pashtun warriors. It is traditionally performed by from 20 to 100 men, outdoors, around a stake or fire. As they dance, the dancers swing guns or swords in their right hands.

Classical Afghan music is similar in style to classical Indian music. Contemporary Western music, especially from the 1970s, is popular with young Afghans. One of the country's most popular singers, Baktash Komran, is also a bodybuilder. He was able to practice his music in a secret underground basement room during the Taliban regime.

USTAD FARIDA MAHWASH

Radio played a powerful role in the modernization of Afghan society in the 1960s and 1970s. Of all the so-called "radio singers" of that period, few have retained their popularity as long as Farida Mahwash has.

She was born into a respectable Kabul family in the 1940s and her mother was a teacher of the Holy Qur'an. Mahwash got a job as a typist at Radio Afghanistan in the early 1960s. When the director of music heard her sing he quickly hired her as a radio performer. Soon Mahwash was one of the most popular of the radio singers, who sang live on the air daily. Their popularity played a critical role in the growing independence of women in Afghan society. Previously, conservative Afghan society viewed women singers as little better than prostitutes.

Mahwash's music was heavily influenced by her mentor, the master instrumentalist and composer Ustad Mohammad Hasham. He wrote many songs for her, including the famed song cycle "O Bacheh" (Oh Boy) that contained a dozen regional Afghan songs.

She became so famous that the Minister of Information bestowed on her the title "Ustad," meaning master musician, in 1977. She was one of the first Afghan women to be so honored.

The great period of radio music, part of a renaissance of the arts in Afghanistan, came to an abrupt end in 1979 when the Soviets invaded. Mahwash remained in Kabul and continued to sing until 1991, when, in fear of her life, she fled to Pakistan. After receiving death threats from the Afghan secret police, who viewed her as a deserter to her country, she was granted political asylum in the United States and today resides in California.

Farida Mahwash continues to perform internationally, often for Afghans in exile. "It's an honor to represent Afghan women whose voices have been suffocated," she said during the Taliban regime.

Art

Traditional Islamic art is nonrepresentational with intricate designs and patterns. The Islamic art of centuries past can be seen in the swirling minarets and splendorous mosques in Afghanistan's cities. Among the most outstanding examples of mosques are the famous Blue Mosque of Mazar-i-Sharif which, according to tradition, contains the tomb of Hazrat

Ali, cousin and son-in-law of the Prophet Muhammad. Its dazzling blue-tiled mosaic entrance and elegant domes make it one of the best-known mosques in the entire Muslim world. Equally celebrated for its artful design is the Friday Mosque (Masjid-i-Jami) in Herat. Another architectural gem is the so-called Mosque of the Sacred Cloak in Kandahar, which is said to be home to a cloak once worn by the Prophet Mohammad.

More ancient, pre-Islamic art includes the Greek and Buddhist stupas, or shrines. The Great Buddha of Bamion stood 180 feet (55 m) tall before it was destroyed by the Taliban rulers on August 2, 2002. Other huge monuments of the past include the Great Arch of Qal'eh-ye Bast and the "Towers of Victory" in Ghazni.

Although much of this early art and architecture is massive, one of the most celebrated Afghanistan art forms are painted miniatures, a style of art that originated there. The country's leading contemporary miniaturist is Haifa Meherzard who refused to flee the country during the Taliban takeover. To spare his artworks from destruction, Meherzd buried many in the ground. When he dug them up again, they were damaged or totally ruined by moisture.

Meherzd has religiously followed the style of the classical miniaturists, including the greatest of them all, Behzad (ca. 1455–ca. 1536) who painted during the golden age of the Timurid dynasty. Meherzd makes no excuses for his devotion to the past. "You in America can innovate because your past is safe," he told one reporter. "Here in Afghanistan, we need to secure our past before we begin to create a future."

Better known to the outside world are Afghanistan's handicrafts, especially their beautiful handmade carpets and rugs with their intricate, complicated patterns and designs. The most revered are the classic Herat carpets dating back to the 16th and 17th centuries. The skilled Afghan artisans are also known for their finely designed jewelry, pottery, woodwork, copper work, and leather goods.

Theater and Cinema

Western-style theater is a relatively new art form in Afghanistan. The first Western plays were produced about 1960 and were adaptations of

European classics. In recent years, Afghan playwrights have produced works about their own people and the challenges of everyday life. These plays have tended to be didactic, teaching audiences lessons in life and morals. Major theaters and theater companies can be found in Kabul, Kandahar, and Herat, while small companies of traveling actors bring live theater to isolated provincial towns.

The first film made in Afghanistan was *Love and Friendship* (1946), a collaboration between Afghan and Indian filmmakers. It was 18 years before another film was made. By 1968, the company Afghan Films began turning out a dozen movies a year, including both feature films and documentaries. Production slowed down drastically during the Soviet-Afghan War and grinded to a complete halt under the Taliban.

The Taliban saw filmmaking and film viewing as equivalent to idolatry. They burned more than a thousand reels of film stock in a bonfire in a Kabul stadium. Fortunately, filmmakers hid the original negatives of most of their films.

The Taliban viewed all arts and entertainment as sinful and frivolous. This movie theater in Kabul reopened in early 2002 after being shut for years by the Taliban. Since the Afghan film industry was also shut down, the theater first showed only foreign films, mostly from India. (UN/DPI Photo by Eskinder Debebe)

Afghan cinemas reopened in November 2001, immediately after the Taliban's fall. However, until very recently there have been no new Afghan films to screen. Most new films are from India, Pakistan, and Iran. The Iranian and Indian film industries have generously given assistance, including necessary equipment, to get Afghan filmmakers back on their feet. The first film to be made here since 1992 was *Scandal* (2003), directed by Seyd Farouq Herbat, a leading Afghan filmmaker, and starring veteran actor Mohammad Eram Khouram, known for his many villainous roles.

"I would just like to act," admits Khouram, "it doesn't really matter what role I get to play."

This desire to get back to work is shared by most of the actors, filmmakers, and other technicians in the Afghan film industry today.

Television and Radio

Before the Taliban came to power Afghanistan's government-run station in Kabul, and nine stations in the provinces, collectively broadcast about five hours of television a day. In 1999, only about 100,000 televisions existed in the entire country.

The Taliban banned television during five years in power. The small television industry has been trying to make up for lost time. Old films, and music and art programs, are popular. In 2002, Afghans were so desperate to be entertained and educated that in Kabul crowds of people gathered around television sets running on car batteries when there is a power failure, a frequent occurrence. In Herat, after the Taliban's fall, shopkeepers were selling television sets they had hidden in storage for up to 10 times their original price, which many eager people were willing to pay.

In the pre-Taliban 1990s, seven AM radio stations and one FM station transmitted programming more than 16 hours a day, broadcasting in Dari, Pashtu, and several other local languages and dialects. In 1999, 167,000 radios existed in the country. The Taliban regime shut down some stations and allowed others to broadcast only Taliban propaganda and religious programs.

Today, radio broadcasts offer poetry reading, music, news, and children's programs. One of the most popular of radio programs is the one-hour news show *Good Morning Afghanistan*, broadcast daily on the government-owned Radio Afghanistan. Its managing editor is Barry Salaam, a former journalism student who previously edited the newsletter of the International Committee of the Red Cross during the Taliban regime. *Good Morning Afghanistan* is an informative and entertaining mixture of news, weather, traffic, sports, and interviews.

"You don't have to use all of your freedom at once," says Salaam, who, like many broadcasters, still fears the possibility of censorship. "We have to go gradually. We have to make people get used to us and the way we do the news. We're very careful with our freedom."

The Press

The first printed newspaper appeared in Afghanistan in 1875. Then, during the reign of King Amanullah, which began in 1919, more than 15 newspapers and magazines were published. In 1962, the *Kabul Times* became the first English-language newspaper. After the Communist coup in 1978 it became a propaganda sheet for the Communist regime and was renamed the *Kabul New Times*. In 1995, there were 15 daily newspapers in Afghanistan, but they were strictly censored when the Taliban came to power a year later.

Since the fall of the Taliban, more than 100 new publications have appeared. They include at least 10 publications aimed at Afghan women, such as the magazine, *Malalai*, whose editor in chief is Jamila Mujahed, Afghanistan's best-known female newscaster. There is even a satirical monthly magazine *Zanbil-e-Gham*, which means "basket of sorrows," first published underground during the Taliban years.

One of the most prominent new periodicals is *Kabul Weekly*, an independent nonpartisan weekly edited by former propaganda filmmaker Fakim Dashty, a relative and close associate of the late mujahideen leader Ahmad Shah Massoud. "Right now is the only real period of freedom of press in Afghanistan," Dashty has said.

Other forms of communications in Afghanistan are limited. In 1996, the country had only 29,000 telephones. Telephone service remains largely restricted to major cities. In 2000, there was only one Internet service provider and few people had personal computers with which to access the Internet.

In general, the arts in Afghanistan have been neglected or suppressed. Much work needs to be done to revive them. For too many years, there has been little time to devote to creating or enjoying poetry, film, theater, and visual art. "We want to export a message of love and cooperation for all the world, and to show our great art," declared Afghan Minister of Information and Culture Said Makhtawn Rahim, "so that people understand this is not just a country of warlords and battle." It is a message that both the world and Afghans themselves need to hear.

NOTES

p. 72 "'Our future depends on . . .'" *New York Times*, March 10, 2002, Arts & Leisure, p. 20.

p. 74 "'Good men are like garnets . . .'" quoted on Afghan-network.net. Available on-line. URL: http://www.afghan-network.net/biographies/khattak.html. Downloaded on December 12, 2002.

p. 75 "'We lost so much . . .'" *New York Times*, March 10, 2002, Arts & Leisure, p. 21.

p. 76 "It's an honor to represent Afghan women . . ." John Baily. "Cry freedom," Guardian Unlimited. Available online. URL: http//www.guardian.co.uk/arts/story/0%2C3604%2C665285%2C00.html. Downloaded on December 12, 2002.

p. 77 "'You in America can innovate . . .'" Guardian Unlimited. As above. p. 20.

p. 79 "'I would just like to act . . .'" Sina Saadi. "Iran's Role in Future of Afghanistan's Cinema." Netiran.com. Available online: URL: http//www.netiran.com/Htdocs/Clippings/Art/020126XXARO1.html. Downloaded on October 28, 2002.

p. 80 "'You don't have to use all of your freedom . . .'" Borzou Daragahi. "A Nascent Free Press Seizes the Moment (Carefully)." Columbia Journalism Review online. Available online. URL: http/www.cjr.org/year/02/4/borzou.asp. Downloaded on February 4, 2003.

p. 80 "'Right now is the only real period of freedom . . .'" Columbia Journalism Review online. As above.

p. 81 "'We want to export a message . . .'" *New York Times*, March 10, 2002, Arts & Leisure, p. 20.

8

DAILY LIFE

Two worlds exist in Afghanistan today. One is the world of war, violence, political instability, and social upheaval. The other is a more peaceful place, where people go about their daily lives, plow their fields, tend their sheep, and share the simple pleasures of life much as their ancestors have for hundreds of years.

These two worlds often exist together on parallel planes. Sometimes the first world intrudes and seriously upsets the second world. Violence and upheaval have at times caused peaceful people to flee from their homes and villages and travel across the border to other lands, often not returning for months or years.

But if anything has helped the Afghan people to survive the terrible events of the past two decades, it is the routine of their daily lives.

"If there is one place [the U.S. invasion of 2001] hasn't gotten to, it's the Afghan home," wrote correspondent Dexter Filkins in the *New York Times*. "It is there where the goodness of the Afghan seems to have survived, protected from the chaos outside."

Village Life

There are 37,000 villages in Afghanistan where more than 85 percent of the population lives. Many villages lie outside of towns and cities, giving the villagers a market where they can sell their crops, livestock, and crafts. But other villages are located in remote valleys and mountain regions, where a person could live his entire life without traveling a distance of more than a few miles. People in such villages rarely see a stranger. News of the outside world reaches there slowly if at all. Life there is far removed from the chaos of Kabul and other cities.

Village life revolves around the home and the workplace, whether it be the field, vineyard, or workshop. Homes are square or rectangular structures with flat brick roofs and walls made of dried mud and straw. Rugs, pillows, and mattresses serve for sitting and sleeping. The mattresses are often stacked away in a corner during the day. Besides the three to four rooms where the family lives, there is often an attached compound that consists of an enclosed area for livestock, sheds for storage, and an open area for cooking.

Electricity and indoor plumbing is still a luxury not found in many Afghan villages. Nearby streams and pools provide water for drinking, bathing, and doing laundry. Cooking is done over a fire fueled by charcoal or the dried dung of animals. In winter, heat is provided by *tawkhansh*, hot-air tunnels that run under the house's floor and are heated at one end by a fire.

Several families may live in one home with several separate units. A typical family unit includes the male head of the household, his wife and children, his brothers, father, mother, cousins, and any unmarried or widowed female relatives. A special room called the *hujra* at the front of the house is used by houseguests and travelers who Afghans welcome with warmth and hospitality, no matter how poor the host may be. "Enter an Afghan's home as a stranger, with dirty boots, unannounced—and as his guest you are his king," wrote Filkins. The *hujra* is also a gathering place in the winter where family members can talk and play games.

Family life in the villages is intensely close knit. Ties run deep and often include all people descended from a common ancestor. If a family member achieves some goal, everyone basks in the glory. If a family member is wronged or hurt, the entire family takes offense. Clan disagreements can quickly lead to violent confrontations and long-standing feuds. Family members take care of one another in times of trouble, relying on themselves and not the damaged infrastructure of the central government.

The father is the unquestioned head of the family. When he dies, his authority is passed on to the eldest son. Women have usually played a subservient role in village life, although they are respected for running the household. This has changed to some degree in the 20th century, especially in urban areas where women have made great advances since the 1960s. The struggle for women's rights will be fully examined in the last chapter of this book.

There are three authority figures in every village, large or small. There is the *malik*, the village headman; the *mirab*, the master of water who determines how it is distributed; and the *mullah*, the Islamic teacher and religious authority (see sidebar, chapter 5). Sometimes the roles of *malik* and *mirab* may be filled by a landowner called *khan*.

Marriage, Afghan Style

Marriage is an extremely serious business for most Afghans. The choosing of the right mate is closely tied to a family's social status, honor, and well-being. Elaborate arrangements are made before an engagement is announced. Great importance is placed on the gifts of money, property, or goods called the brideprice, which is given to the bride's family by the groom's family. It is usually equaled in value by the dowry the bride's family gives to the couple, which includes everything from clothing to homemade household utensils made by the bride and her friends.

Many marriages in the rural areas are between cousins. In urban areas, where the population is more fluid, marriages between non-relatives, or even between members of different ethnic groups, are not uncommon. Typically, females in their teens marry males in their mid-twenties. However, the high cost of the bridesprice has made it difficult for many young men to marry. They may put off marriage until they have acquired enough wealth and property. This has led to many marriages between young girls and much older, prosperous men. These men often die within a few years, leaving behind young, well-off widows.

Polygamy is allowed under Islamic religious law, but is increasingly rare in Afghanistan. The expense of keeping more than one wife is prohibitive for the average Afghan man. The most common reason for a man to seek a second wife is if his first wife is barren or has not produced a male child.

Dress

In the larger towns and cities, Afghans may wear Western clothes, but in the villages people dress in the traditional Afghan garb. Men wear long cotton shirts that reach to their knees, and full-length, baggy cotton pants. Each man wears a skullcap on his head, usually covered by a turban. The style of the turban often tells what tribe or ethnic group he belongs to. In the winter, men wear long woolen coats called *capins*, and sometimes replace the turban with a warm cap made of lambskin.

Afghan women wear long, full-bodied dresses and cover their hair with cloth shawls that can also be pulled down over their faces in the presence of strangers. Under traditional Islamic law, women are not supposed to show their hair or face in public.

Women were formerly required by law to wear a *burka*, a long, sacklike garment that covered them from head to toe whenever they might come in contact with male strangers, especially in cities. In 1959, the government made the *burka* optional for women and many discarded the unwieldy covering. Under the Taliban it once again became mandatory. Today, more and more Afghan women, especially in the cities, are abandoning the *burka*.

Food and Drink

Afghan cuisine is an intriguing blend of the cuisines of the various people who have invaded and conquered the country over many centuries. Iranian and Indian food are the dominating influences, although Afghan dishes are milder than their spicy Indian counterparts.

As might be expected in such an impoverished country, bread and rice are staples of the diet. The national bread is naan, a round, flat unleavened bread that is baked in a clay pot buried underground to retain its heat. Naan also serves as an eating utensil to pick up other food. Otherwise, it is customary to eat food not with a knife and fork but with the fingers of the right hand.

Rice mixed with meat, such as beef, goat, or chicken, or vegetables is called *pilau*. *Pilau* is such a universal dish in Afghanistan that the word has come to mean any kind of food for many Afghans. In the north, however, noodles are more popular than rice, especially an Afghan variation on ravioli called *ashak*.

A typical dessert is fresh fruit—cherries, plums, or apricots—or nuts. Desserts for more special occasions include *faluda*, a pudding steamed for 12 hours in a bag that is served with syrup and boiled rice, and *jelabi*, deep-fried pieces of wheat bread coated with syrup.

Alcohol is frowned upon in this Muslim country, so the national drink is tea. Green tea is popular in the north, and black tea is popular in the south. Afghans like their tea sweet or spicy. They often add sugar or cardamom (a spice) to tea. Some even drink their tea with a sugar cube in their mouth.

Tea drinking can be a highly social activity. In teahouses, men gather to drink steaming cups of tea and talk about the events of the day. Most villages have at least one teahouse, and cities are full of them.

THE NOMADS: LIFE ON THE MOVE

Not all Afghans live in permanent homes. Perhaps 10 percent of the population are nomads or semi-nomads. They follow their herds of sheep, goats, and other animals as they graze in low-lying winter settlements to summer pastures in the higher elevations. True nomads live constantly on the move, pitching tents made of black goats' hair whenever they stop. They travel at a speed of three to 15 miles a day, the younger men following the sheep and goats on the highland trails, and the other men leading the women, children, and elderly with camels and donkeys on lower trails.

But most of these herding clans are not true nomads. They travel with their livestock part of the year and return to their portable homes, called yurts, in the fall and winter. Yurts, built on a wood frame and covered with woven reeds, can be disassembled when needed.

Living on the move is hard, but these people take great pride in it. They play an indispensable role in the lives of the villagers, selling them meat, animals, wool, and skins and buying grains and household items on their twice-yearly visits. The nomads also spread news that they have picked up in their travels.

Sports and Recreation

Afghans have always taken sports seriously. Trained to be warriors, they have brought the same fiercely competitive spirit to their games. Winning is an emblem of honor an athlete carries for himself, his family, and his tribe.

It is not surprising that the national sport is the rough and tumble game of *buzkashi* (see sidebar). The other sport Afghans are most passionate about is a form of wrestling called *pablwani*. The rules allow a wrestler to grab onto an opponent's clothing and arms. By the end of a match, both wrestlers are often nearly naked with their clothes ripped to shreds.

Afghans' abilities in wrestling and weight lifting have taken them to the Olympic Games. In 2000, however, they were not allowed to participate, because of international condemnation of the Taliban's oppressive reign. The Taliban also banned women from participating in sports, and forced male athletes to wear cumbersome long pants and long-sleeved shirts. The Olympic Stadium in Kabul was used as a site for public executions.

The new government is anxious to revive sports teams, especially for women. A new Afghan National Olympic Committee is working hard to assemble competitive teams for the 2004 Olympic Games in Athens, Greece. The Committee is working on a women's volleyball team, but it has had trouble getting women to join. Even before the Taliban, Afghan women were not encouraged to participate in sports. "Without the permission of their husbands, many won't do it," said Olympic Committee Chairman Sayed Mahmood Zia Dashti. "It doesn't matter what we say."

Volleyball, soccer, and basketball are popular today and were introduced in Afghanistan after World War II. Other Western-style sports such as tennis, golf, and the English game of cricket, were brought over by King Habibullah in the 1910s as part of his campaign to Westernize his country.

Holidays

The hardships of everyday life amid war, strife, drought, and famine, have made holidays in Afghanistan even more important.

BUZKASHI—AFGHANISTAN'S NATIONAL SPORT

Imagine two teams on horseback vying to seize the headless carcass of a calf and carry it across a goal line. *Buzkashi* may sound grotesque to Americans, but it is an honorable sport in Afghanistan.

This rugged game first developed on the Mongolian plains of central Asia where the carcass used was that of a goat. The word *buzkashi* literally means "get the goat." While some teams are small, some consist of hundreds of men.

The two teams on horseback encircle the carcass on the playing field. When a signal is given, the players, still mounted, move into the center and attempt to lift the carcass onto their horses. In Qarajai, one kind of *buzkashi,* the rider who gets the carcass must carry it around a marker and then bring it to the team's designated scoring area. In Tudabarai, another variation, the rider with the carcass must carry it away from the starting circle and stay free of the other riders. It may sound dangerous, but the horses and their riders are so skilled that injuries are rare. One game lasts an hour, with a 10-minute break at halftime.

Two buzkashi *teams fight for the headless carcass of a calf, which they must carry into a circle to score in this age-old national sport.* (AP/Wide World Photos/Murad Sezer)

The Persian New Year, which takes place on the first day of spring, was banned by the Taliban because it was not a religious holiday and it predates Islamic times. It was finally celebrated again in grand style in March 2002 in Mazar-i-Sharif's famous Blue Mosque. President Hamid Karzai spoke for all his people when he declared in a speech that day, "In this new year, God willing, complete peace will come to Afghanistan."

The other prominent secular holiday is Independence Day, commemorating the country's independence in 1919 following the Third Anglo-Afghan War. Although the war actually ended in May, the holiday is celebrated in August, the time of harvest in most rural areas, giving the Afghans two good reasons to celebrate.

Most other holidays are Islamic feasts and festivals. Ramadan, the ninth month of the Islamic calendar, is the Muslim month of fasting and prayer. It culminates in Eid al-Fitr, a three-day-long feast that includes prayers at the mosque and visits to the homes of relatives and friends. Eid al-Adha, the Festival of Sacrifice, is celebrated on the 10th day of the

Afghan women celebrate the Persian New Year in Mazar-i-Sharif in March 2002. The holiday, that marks the start of spring, was banned during the Taliban's reign. (AP/Wide World Photos/Alexander Zemlianichenko)

12th month of the Muslim calendar. It is a commemoration of the prophet Abraham's willingness to sacrifice everything for God, even his own son. The festival includes the blood sacrifice of animals, a portion of which is given to the poor.

Education

The hunger for learning throughout Afghanistan today is more intense than it has ever been. Literacy classes for adults, particularly women, are held in crumbling basement rooms, halls, and neighbor's houses in every city and many towns. Both boys and girls trudge through war-scarred landscapes to primitive mud schoolrooms where they sit on the floor often without enough materials or textbooks to go around. Few complain, however, because the right to attend school is a great privilege. It was completely denied to girls and women under the puritanical laws of the Taliban.

Even before the Taliban's repression, Afghanistan's education system had long been neglected. It has one of the highest adult illiteracy rates in Asia, if not the world. In 1990, a United Nations study estimated that 70 percent of all adults over the age of 25 could not read or write. In 2000, the last full year of Taliban rule, only one out of three boys attended school, while only three out of 100 girls did so, mostly in secret.

Education was not a high priority in this country of farmers and shepherds until the 20th century. Before then, the only schools were religious ones run in mosques and open only to boys. What little education girls received they got at home, mostly from the older women.

In 1903, in Kabul, King Habibullah established the first modern secondary school that taught both religious and secular subjects. Under his successor, King Amanullah, more schools were built, including a girls' school, which opened in the capital in 1929. The 1931 constitution called for compulsory and free elementary schooling for children. The first Western-style institution of higher learning was a medical school established in Kabul in 1932. By 1946 it had evolved into Kabul University and began admitting women students in 1960. A second institute of higher learning, the University of Nangashar, opened in Jalalabad in 1964. The Polytechnic Institute, funded by the Soviets, opened in Kabul in 1969. During the 1980s, the Soviets helped establish universities at Balkh, Herat, and Kandahar. Kabul also boasts a military academy for army officers, a vocational school, and teachers' college.

More and more Afghans see education as a necessary tool in rebuilding their country and making it prosperous. Many educated and professional Afghans fled during the Communist and Taliban regimes. As some of them return, they will help strengthen an educational system that is sorely lacking in teachers, books, and other basic materials.

Students at the recently reopened Kabul University were so frustrated by poor conditions, including dormitories without water or electricity, that they rioted in mid-November 2002. One thousand students marched towards the president's office to express their grievances, vandalizing shops and parked cars along the way. Security forces responded with violence, and four people were killed in two days of rioting. The one positive outcome of the incident was that President Karzai promised to improve university conditions.

Adults going back to school to learn to read and write have few complaints.

"I have no knowledge, and so I am not a useful person," admits one 45-year-old widow with six children attending literacy classes. "If I can get some knowledge, I can help my children more." Afghans hope that their children will go on to college and become the doctors, lawyers, teachers, and other professionals that their homeland desperately needs to rebuild itself. This next generation of educated Afghans holds the promise of a better future for this decimated nation.

NOTES

p. 82 "'If there is one place . . .'" *New York Times,* November 18, 2001, Week in Review, p. 7.

p. 83 "'Enter an Afghan's home . . .'" *New York Times,* November 18, 2001, Week in Review, p. 7.

p. 87 "'Without the permission of their husbands . . .'" *New York Times,* January 27, 2002, p. 12.

p. 89 "'In this new year . . .'" *New York Times,* March 22, 2002, p. A12.

p. 91 "'I have no knowledge . . .'" *New York Times,* September 22, 2002, p. 1.

9

THE CITIES

Only 15 percent of Afghanistan's population live in cities. Only five cities have a population of more than 100,000, but they are important centers of the nation's commercial, cultural, and administrative activities. Afghanistan's cities are rich historically, too, dating back 2,000 to 3,000 years.

These bustling metropolises sprang up at the major intersections of trade routes, near rivers, and by strategic mountain passes. They have survived centuries of pillaging, warfare, and near total destruction at the hands of many conquerors and invaders. The cities have an indomitable spirit. Plagued by the strife of the past two decades, Afghanistan's cities are rising once again.

Kabul—Capital City

If any city can be said to encompass Afghanistan's long, often agonizing history, it is Kabul (pop. 2,206,300, 2003 est.). Kabul has existed, on several sites, for more than 3,000 years. It has been built up and torn down several times. It has been the capital of a mighty empire and, for the past two and a quarter centuries, has served as the capital of Afghanistan. And while its population has fluctuated greatly in the 1980s and 1990s, Kabul remains Afghanistan's largest city. People have flocked here to escape the warfare in the countryside, and then fled to other countries when the fighting came to Kabul.

Kabul has been important because of its location. Kabul is situated on a sheltered plateau nearly 6,000 feet above sea level in east central Afghanistan. It sits on the Kabul River and between two mountain ranges. Highways link the city with nearly every province in the country.

In early times, the city was central in trade and commerce between Afghans and Indians. It remained overshadowed by Herat to the west, the cultural and commercial center of the Persian Empire in the 14th and 15th centuries. That changed in 1504 when the conqueror Babur made Kabul capital of his Moghul Empire. Although the capital moved to Delhi 22 years later, Kabul remained an important Moghul city until 1738 when Persian conqueror Nadir Shah seized it.

In 1747, Kabul became part of newly independent Afghanistan, and in 1773 it replaced Kandahar as the capital. Its proximity to the Khyber Pass, the natural gateway to India, made it a focal point for the competing nations of Great Britain, Russia, and Persia through the early decades of the 19th century.

British troops, anxious to block the corridor to British India, occupied Kabul during the First Anglo-Afghan War (1839–1842). In 1842, when fleeing British troops were massacred by Afghans, their comrades retaliated by burning part of the city. The British occupied Kabul again in 1879, during the Second Anglo-Afghan War.

Kabul was the model city for the modernization movement after World War II. New factories and plants made it Afghanistan's first industrial center, although a relatively minor one by Western standards. Artists, writers, intellectuals, and musicians gave the city a sophisticated and cosmopolitan air from the 1950s through the 1970s that was not found anywhere else in the country. Kabul's "golden age" ended with the Soviet Invasion in December 1979. Shattered by war, Kabul was battered again by the civil war that followed the Soviet withdrawal in 1989.

When the Taliban took the city in 1996 after two years of warfare, they were at first welcomed as champions of order and peace. But the security they brought to a war-torn metropolis had a high price. The Taliban looked on the cosmopolitan atmosphere of Kabul as thoroughly decadent and stamped it out. The city and its residents suffered harshly under the Taliban's puritanical rule. No city rejoiced more than when the

A young boy carries fresh bread to market against a background of gleaming white houses in one of Kabul's crowded residential neighborhoods.
(United Nations)

combined forces of the United States and the Northern Alliance drove the Taliban out in late 2001.

Here is one American reporter's impression of Kabul at that historic moment:

> Withered old men carry bundles of firewood strapped to their shoulders. Shrouded women move through the bazaars like downtrodden ghosts. . . . Only with a second look comes the sights that would have been unthinkable a month ago. Over there, some men are clean-shaven. . . . Over here are a few courageous women, walking outdoors without the head-to-toe burka.

Today Kabul is coming back to life, reasserting its importance as Afghanistan's leading administrative and cultural center. The ancient and the modern co-exist dramatically in Kabul. The old city with its narrow, crooked streets and crowded bazaars still exist on the south bank in the shadow of tall, modern offices and apartment buildings.

Despite the devastation of years of war, Kabul has retained some of its charm and beauty. Impressive cultural landmarks are Babur's tomb and its surrounding gardens, once famous throughout Asia, the mausoleum of Nader Shah, and the Minar-i-Istiklal (Column of Independence), built to commemorate the new nation of Afghanistan in 1919. The Dar ul-Amaan Palace now houses the parliamentary and government offices, while the fort of Bala Hissar is now a military college. The nation's largest and oldest institute of higher learning, Kabul University, is here, as is the recently reopened National Gallery, Afghanistan's largest fine art museum. Some landmarks, such as the famous blue dome of the Jhaji Yaqub Mosque, have suffered damage in the years of war, but are still standing.

If Afghanistan is to join the ranks of modern Asian nations with secure and stable governments, the first signs of its success will be seen here, in its capital city.

Kandahar—Afghanistan's Second City

Kandahar (also spelled "Qandahar") is located on a fertile plain in southern Afghanistan, (pop. 339,300, 2003 est.) and is Afghanistan's second-largest city. According to legend, Alexander the Great founded it on the site of another city as he passed through on the way to conquer India. This is supported by its very name, a corruption of "Iskander," the Asian word for "Alexander."

A number of cities have existed on the site since Alexander's time. Kandahar's so-called Old City is something of a misnomer because it was founded relatively recently. In 1747, Ahmad Shah Durrani, Afghanistan's first emir, was crowned near Kandahar and later made it his capital. Durrani's mausoleum is a major historical site.

Perhaps Kandahar's darkest days were after the Taliban seized it in 1994 and made it their stronghold during their short but brutal reign. The city was one of the last to fall to the Northern Alliance and United States forces in late 2001. It was heavily bombed.

Members of the 82nd Airborne stationed in Kandahar take a break from the dangerous work of hunting for Taliban and al-Qaeda members hiding in the villages of southeastern Afghanistan. (Photo courtesy of John Otfinoski)

The Kandahar Airport, already heavily damaged from the Soviet-Afghan War, was further damaged in 2001. Said to be the largest airport in Central Asia, it was build with money and expertise from the United States, and, as of early 2003, U.S. forces were still using the airfield to hunt down remaining Taliban and al-Qaeda fighters in the desert nearby.

Lying at the junction of several ancient trading routes, Kandahar remains, despite the setbacks of war, Afghanistan's chief trade and commercial center. Surrounded by a richly irrigated farming area, it is the central market for farmers bringing in their tobacco, fruits, and other crops. Kandahar grapes are noted for their fine quality throughout the world. The city is also a manufacturing center for woolen clothes, silk, and cotton goods, and a hub for the canning, drying, and packing of fruit.

Among the greatest landmarks of the old city is the Kherqa Sharif, a shrine containing the cloak of the prophet Muhammad, Afghanistan's most sacred relic. Another highlight is the Chel Zina, 40 steps leading to a rock chamber that contains an inscription by Babur listing all the domains under his power.

The adjoining modern section of Kandahar is the principal urban center of the Pashtun people in Afghanistan and boasts textile factories and a technical college.

Herat—Afghanistan's Persian Jewel

Situated on the Harirud River in northwestern Afghanistan near the Iranian border, Herat (pop. 171,500, 2003 est.) was another casualty of the Soviet–Afghan War and the civil war that followed it. The city suffered less devastation during the U.S.–Taliban War and served as a gathering place for refugees fleeing the fighting in the east. From here they fled across the border into Iran.

Herat's history is more prominently on display than that of either Kabul or Kandahar. With its ancient moat, city gates, and magnificent minarets, Herat is considered the most beautiful of ancient Afghan cities. For much of its long history Herat was part of the Persian Empire, and a center for Persian art, literature, and architecture in the 15th and 16th centuries. Herat only became a permanent part of Afghanistan in 1863. The Soviets installed a military command headquarters there during the 1980s.

Herat is located in the fertile Hari Rud valley, one of Afghanistan's most agriculturally productive regions. The area is rich in grain, fruits, nuts, vegetables, and sheep. It is the central marketplace for these products as well as the center of the Afghan textile and carpet industries. For many years it was also the center of the *burka* industry. Sales have plummeted, however, since the fall of the Taliban, as many Afghan women are abandoning the *burka* for more comfortable, modern clothing.

With the help of U.S. aid, Herat's ancient buildings, damaged by erosion and the war, are being lovingly restored. The great mosque, the Masjide Jami, which has been a center of Muslim worship since the sixth century B.C., is almost completely restored. The glorious complex, built in the late 1400s by Queen Gawhar Shad, Tamberlane's daughter-in-law, still stands, although only six of its 12 original minarets remain. These six are being reconstructed through a UN building project.

The modern city of Herat has grown up around the old city's walls and is the main trading center for exports going to Iran and Turkmenistan. A majority of Herat's population are Tajiks. There are also large numbers of Turkmans and Uzbeks.

Mazar-i-Sharif—Northern Afghanistan's Capital

The largest city in northern Afghanistan, Mazar-i-Sharif (pop. 246,900, 2003 est.) was one of the first areas the Soviets seized when they entered the country in 1979. They established a military command there in 1981, and build a new road and rail bridge across the Amu Danya river. When the Soviets withdrew 10 years later, the Northern Alliance took over the area and the city remained their stronghold through the coming civil war and much of the fight against the Taliban. On August 8, 1998, the Taliban captured Mazar-i-Sharif and the Northern Alliance troops fled to the countryside. The city became the scene of some of the worst atrocities of the war, as the Taliban systematically detained and executed civilians, especially Hazaras, an ethnic group. Hundreds of Hazara prisoners were transported from the city in large metal containers and died of asphyxiation en route to another prison.

While the city suffered under the Taliban, the surrounding area also suffered drought and famine. Since the war ended in late 2001, Marzar-i-Sharif has been the focal point for international relief efforts in the north, the poorest region of this impoverished nation. Some 27 separate relief camps in the city were serving residents as of March 2002.

The city's name means "tomb of the saint" and refers to Muhammad's son-in-law Ali, whose grave was supposedly discovered here in the 12th or 15th century 13 miles from the city. The blue-tiled mosque and shrine that mark the tomb's location, is a place of pilgrimage for Muslims, especially Shi'ites, who venerate Ali and his family as Muhammed's lawful successors.

Like Herat, Mazar-i-Sharif only became part of Afghanistan in the mid-19th century. However, it has been an important Muslim center for centuries. A famous Islamic theological school is also located there. Mazar-i-Sharif has a thriving economy built on carpet making and the cotton and silk industries.

The Blue Mosque, Afghanistan's biggest mosque, is an important pilgrim destination and cultural landmark of Mazar-i-Sharif. (AP/Wide World Photos/Efrem Lukatsky)

Strategic Jalalabad

Sitting just to the west of the Khyber Pass, Jalalabad (pop. 163,600, 2003 est.) is one of the country's youngest cities. The site of an ancient Buddhist city, it has long been a defensive and military center for Afghanistan. Around 1560, Babur, founder of the Mogul Empire, chose it to be his base of operation. The town was built a decade later by Babur's grandson, Jalabiddi Ahb, who named it after himself. The British held the city in 1842 during the First Anglo-Afghan War.

Jalalabad has had a reputation as a haven for smugglers, bandits, and thieves, who thrived for centuries in the surrounding mountain passes. The Taliban ended much of the crime and corruption, but with their fall, crime is again on the rise. The local warlords are involved with the racketeering, smuggling, and stealing.

But all this has not stopped people from coming to Jalalabad from other towns and cities. Eighteen-year-old Ahmad Fawad, a carpenter, made the journey from Kabul in late 2001 because he heard Jalalabad was more peaceful. "Almost all the homes where I live were destroyed starting when I was about 10 years old," he told a reporter. "That's how it goes here. I have not seen peace in my whole life. From childhood, I have seen blood, bullets, guns, nothing else. If there is peace, and they want me to build houses, I'm ready to work night and day."

Jalalabad is also an important trading center with neighboring Pakistan and India. The surrounding area produces rice and sugarcane. The sugar is processed and refined in Jalalabad, which also has a thriving papermaking industry. It is home to Jalalabad University and a medical school.

LASHKAR GAH—AFGHANISTAN'S "LITTLE AMERICA"

West of Kandahar, on the Helmand River in southern Afghanistan, there is a reminder of better times when U.S. goodwill and aid first made a difference. In the 1950s, Americans were sent there to work on the 300-foot high Kajuki Dam, which helped irrigate the region. They also built a model community that they called Bast after an ancient city whose ruins lay nearby. But to Afghans it was Lashkar Gah, nicknamed "Little America."

At Lashkar Gah the Americans built a modern hospital, the best equipped in the entire country and a high school where Americans taught the local children. They also operated a nursery school for the local people.

Then came the Soviet invasion of 1979. The Americans left and "Little America" has never been the same. Drought dried up the rivers used for irrigation, and the hospital, while still operating, was neglected as were Afghanistan's other medical facilities (see chapter 10).

"From that time [1979] until now, there has been nothing good here," said Abdul Aziz, a hospital engineer. Now, with the return of the Americans, Afghans hope that "Little America," will rise again, and that American aid and expertise will play even a larger role of helping them get back on their feet.

The Ancient Glories of Ghazni

While Ghazni (pop. 40,200, 2003 est.) is known today as the place where the famous Afghan sheepskin coats are made, it once was one of Asia's most beautiful cities. Eighty miles south of Kabul, Ghazni reached its greatest glory between A.D. 994 and 1160 when it was the capital of the Turkish Ghaznivid dynasty and controlled most of northern India, Persia, and Central Asia. Mahmud of Ghazni built the mosque called the Celestial Bride, considered today one of the finest examples of its architectural period.

Ghazni's golden age ended when the kings of Ghor sacked it in 1149. Its final downfall came 70 years later when Ogotai, one of Genghis Khan's sons, pillaged it. A new city was later built south of the Old Ghazni, whose only identifiable ruins are two high towers. It became part of the kingdom of Afghanistan in 1737, and was held by the British in 1839 and 1842, during the First Anglo-Afghan War.

Modern Ghazni is a market center not only for valuable lambskins, but also corn, fruit, wool, and camel's haircloth. Most of Ghazni's residents are Tajiks.

NOTES
p. 94 "'Withered old men carry bundles . . .'" *New York Times*, December 2, 2001, p. B4.
p. 100 "'Almost all the homes . . .'" *New York Times*, November 25, 2001, p. B10.
p. 100 "'From that time [1979] until now . . .'" *New York Times*, March 15, 2002, p. A4.

10

PROBLEMS AND SOLUTIONS

There is no shortage of problems in Afghanistan, but practical, workable solutions are harder to come by. Some problems go back centuries. Others developed more recently. None of them will be easy to solve and their solutions will take money, resources, determination, and cooperation.

When discussing the many problems facing Afghans today, it is best to prioritize. Some immediate needs must be met: food, shelter, medical care must be provided to impoverished Afghans. Afterwards, less immediate, but equally important problems, can be tackled.

Hunger

Lack of food has long been a problem here. Farmers and their families cannot usually survive on what they grow. More recently the problem of hunger has reached catastrophic proportions. Warfare has disrupted the growing and harvesting cycle. Farmers have fled the countryside to escape being caught in the crossfire. A series of droughts from 1997 to 2002 has further worsened the situation.

Today, families are so desperate for food that some fathers sell their children at the bazaar in exchange for a monthly allotment. Akhtar Muhammad, a poor farmer in Kangori, a town in the mountainous north, sold two of his 10 children to another man at a bazaar for bags of wheat. "What else could I do?" he told a reporter. "I miss my sons, but there was nothing to eat."

Most children sold this way live in a state of bonded labor. They are not considered full members of their new families and have few rights.

Other Afghan families deal with hunger by foraging for whatever food they can find. Some are reduced to eating boiled grass, while still others combine the grass with a little barley to bake into a crude, barely edible bread.

International relief organizations, such as the World Food Program of the United Nations, have been crucial in feeding thousands of starving Afghans. But these organizations are keenly aware that centrally located food camps are only a temporary solution to a monumental problem. To assure a new harvest when the droughts end, people need to return to their villages and towns, resume their lives, and start growing crops. They also need to be taught to accept new methods of agriculture, to use more modern equipment, and to plant better seeds that will increase their meager yield. In the past, Afghan farmers have stubbornly resisted such new technology and methods. It is the task of the new government to convince them the old ways cannot feed a nation of nearly 28 million people.

In the meantime, the immediate challenge for relief workers is to convince people to leave the relief camps where they are fed. Once they are able to return to their farms, they can prepare for the next planting season. "If you just give away food, you undermine the economy," said Mireille Borne of the aid group Acted. "You have to think about the long term."

Lawlessness

For too long, Afghanistan has been a lawless land. From September through November 2002, there were no fewer than three assassination attempts on the life of President Karzai. In February and July of the same year, two top government officials were assassinated. None of these crimes have been fully solved but al-Qaeda is rumored to have been involved in them. When one of Karzai's would-be assassins was killed, he was identified as an al-Qaeda sympathizer.

The government must make the cities and countryside safe for everyone. This is not only critical in gaining the confidence of the populace, but it is a crucial part of convincing foreign businesses, investors, and tourists to come and invest in Afghanistan.

Widespread corruption also contributes to lawlessness, particularly corruption among the provincial warlords and their underlings. For them, everything and everyone has its price, and nothing is sacred. In 2002, American reporters in Jalalabad, one of the country's most corrupt cities, were surprised to learn the rice they were being sold at their hotel had originally been given to the needy by international relief aid and then snatched up by local warlords to be sold for profit.

Many warlords set their own laws, running cities and whole provinces as their private fiefdoms. Some of the worst offenders have been rejected by their people and lost their power, but many others still operate freely. President Karzai hopes that by bringing warlords into the government and reforming them, he will move effectively deal with their corruption, while uniting the country.

For the short term, United States and international peacekeeping troops are the best means of keeping some law and order in Afghanistan. But with about 5,500 troops in the country, this task is nearly impossible. The peacekeepers are mostly limited to patrolling Kabul and securing the safety of President Karzai and his government. According to Morton Halperin, a senior fellow at the Council on Foreign Relations, the war-torn country of Bosnia in Eastern Europe had 60,000 peacekeeping troops serving in the early 1990s, and Afghanistan is 12 times larger than Bosnia.

The long-term solution is to form a standing army and a national police force, both loyal to the government. President Karzai has made a national army and police force a top priority of his administration but both are still in the early stages of development. In the meantime, the foreign peacekeepers must do their best to maintain order in a lawless land.

The Opium Trade

The continuing and highly profitable trade in opium is an ongoing problem for Afghanistan. It starts in the poppy fields of the northern provinces, where the poppies are picked. They are then driven in trucks to the drug factories on the Pakistani border where the opium derived from the poppies is refined into heroin for international export.

Not even the Taliban with their draconian laws and harsh justice could stamp out the drug trafficking. Their ban on poppy growing in 2000, under strong pressure from the United States, slowed down the trade, but it gained momentum in the chaotic days that followed the Taliban's fall. Now the Karzai government is facing similar pressure from the West to stop the flow of drugs from Afghanistan or risk losing some of the billions in aid promised to rebuild the country.

To help persuade the Afghan farmers who grow poppies to return to legal crops, the United States and the World Bank gave the government $80 million to distribute as an incentive in 2002. Unfortunately, much of this money found its way into the treasure chests of local warlords, whose top priority is rebuilding their own power bases.

In August 2002, United Nations' observers admitted frankly that the four-month program of money distribution had largely failed to end the poppy problem. The 2002 crop was one of the largest since the late 1990s, and was worth as much as $1 billion for the local economy.

Men harvest poppies near Kandahar, the source of Afghanistan's illegal but most profitable exports—opium and heroin. Government efforts to eradicate the fields, although supported by the United States, have so far not been successful. (AP/Wide World Photos/Victor R. Caivano)

In a country as poor as Afghanistan, such money is hard to resist. "We don't do this because we like it," confessed Jamul, a local poppy farmer, "we know it is wrong, but we are poor . . ." Until the Afghan government is strong enough to end the corruption, reign in the warlords, and meet the basic needs of its people, Afghanistan's dubious distinction as the world's number-one producer of raw opium will likely remain unchallenged.

Roads

Of Afghanistan's 13,041 miles (21,000 kilometers) of roads, only about 17 percent are in good condition. Two decades of war have damaged or destroyed most of them, making travel in many parts of the country nearly impossible. This has become a major problem not only for the transportation of people and goods within the country but also for trading between Afghanistan and its neighbors.

In September 2002, U.S. president George W. Bush pledged $180 million for a road improvement project that would involve United States, Saudi Arabia, and Japan. "We'll help develop a modern infrastructure so that the Afghan entrepreneur will be able to move products from one city to the next and so that people will be able to find work, they'll be able to put food on the table," Bush said at a joint appearance with President Karzai at the United Nations in New York City.

In November, work began on the restoration of Afghanistan's 1,490 miles (2,400 km) of "ring roads," so called because they connect the country's major cities, and another 435 miles (700 km) of roads that link Afghanistan to Iran, Pakistan, Uzbekistan, Turkmenistan, and Tajikistan.

It is estimated that it will take $650 million of foreign aid and lots of foreign expertise to complete this ambitious project. Road repair is one problem that Afghanistan seems to be solving. Many observers believe that reopening Afghanistan's roads will be a major step towards improving the country's economy and overall well-being.

Health Care

At present, Afghanistan is one of the unhealthiest nations on Earth. Few countries have as poor and dysfunctional a health care system. The average life expectancy is 44 years—some 30 years less than the average life expectancy in the United States. More than one in five Afghan children die before the age of five. Hygiene and medical care is so abysmal that more women die giving birth than from any other cause. Conditions are the worst in the northeastern provinces, where one foreign researcher compared them to those of "biblical times, some 2,000 years ago."

According to United Nations' statistics, there are 1,038 health care facilities for a population of 27 million which means just one hospital for every 26,000 people. Only half of those facilities have safe drinking water, and only 27 percent have electricity. There are only 200 doctors to care for 4.5 million people in southern Afghanistan. Hospitals, when they exist at all, are in terrible shape. Medical equipment no longer works. Hospital beds have no sheets. Patients lucky enough to be admitted must bring their own food, medicine, and blood. Fresh blood for transfusions is so hard to come by that it is sold in the bazaar at $150 for 500cc, a price far beyond the means of the average Afghan. Doctors cannot diagnose diseases properly because they lack the necessary tools. The diseases that most often go untreated are malaria, measles, cholera, tuberculosis, and malnutrition.

Training men and women for health care work is critical. The United States has promised to build a medical clinic in Kabul for this purpose. Information and instructions about hygiene must be spread through the work of government agencies. The U.S. secretary of health and human services, Tommy G. Thompson, put it bluntly during a visit to Afghanistan health facilities in October 2002: "The Taliban have devastated the land and its medical infrastructure. The Afghans have nothing, they need virtually everything."

Women's Rights

The Afghans whose health is most at risk are women. Women of child-bearing age are especially vulnerable because pregnancy is often life-threatening in this country of poverty and poor health care. Afghan women today also face many other problems. They can recall a time not long ago when they had meaningful lives, jobs, and a respected position in society. For example, in 1964, women participated in drafting the famous constitution. And, through the early 1990s, women worked as

Afghan girls at the Zarghuna School in Kabul are eager for the education that was denied them under the Taliban. Reopening in early 2002, the school has more than 2,600 girls from age seven to 20 enrolled as students. (UN/DPI Photo by Eskinder Debebe)

doctors, lawyers, politicians, and other professionals, making up a large percentage of the work force. Their presence was as much out of necessity—to cover for the men at war—as it was a conscious liberation movement. In pre-Taliban years, 70 percent of teachers and 40 percent of doctors in Kabul were women.

This all came to an abrupt end when the Taliban assumed power. Religious extremists had a twisted interpretation of the Qur'an in which they viewed women as sinful and inferior beings that must be subjugated. They forced women of every age and educational level back into the home. "For adult women like me, our houses had become our prisons because the Taliban said we could not go outside unaccompanied by a male relative," recalled 27-year-old Shahnaz Rasoul, who today is a medical student at Kabul University. "We were barely alive."

"Our life under the Taliban is really disgusting," said another women while the Taliban were still in power. "Sometimes I come to the conclusion that there is no way but to commit suicide, but then I feel what will happen to my children and then I scold myself."

Since the fall of the Taliban women's lives have improved, but there are still many obstacles for women who want to return to work and advance their lives. Conservative attitudes dominate this traditional, male-dominated society. Many of the same Islamic mullahs and local warlords who oppose secularization and a central government, also oppose greater rights for women.

SIMA SAMAR (b. 1957)

Afghan women probably have no more passionate advocate for their rights than their Human Rights Commissioner Sima Samar.

An ethnic Hazara, Samar was born in February 1957 in Ghazni. As a young medical student she belonged to the Revolutionary Afghan Women's Association, a feminist group. Her first husband was killed during the Soviet invasion of 1979. She fled to Pakistan, where she cared for Afghans in a refugee camp. In 1987, Samar opened a hospital for women in Quetta, Pakistan. It was the first hospital in Pakistan that was staffed entirely by women. Two years later, Samar returned to Afghanistan and established a nonprofit organization that ran four hospitals, 10 clinics, and rural schools for 22,000 Afghan boys and girls. The Taliban's death threats and intimidation tactics did not deter her from her mission.

When the new government was set up under Hamid Karzai in December 2001, Samar was named Minister of Women's Affairs in the Council of Ministers. When the transitional government was elected in June 2002, she was appointed Human Rights Commissioner.

Sima Samar believes that Afghan women must be brought into the workplace quickly through short-term management, accounting, and computer training courses.

"We need to create job opportunities to give them [women] confidence and give them their pride back," she has said. Although her goals are high, Samara is realistic about the long way women have to go in this conservative Muslim nation. "It takes time to change things," she has admitted. "It won't happen overnight." But thanks to courageous, hardworking women like Sima Samar, it will happen eventually.

One way for women to rise above this reactionaryism is through education. While about 60 percent of the students at Kabul University were women in the 1970s, this figure dropped to less than 10 percent in the late 1900s. In 2002, some 1,500 women took the university's entrance exam. Many of them wanted to study to be teachers and to help other women to become full members of their society.

One of the most promising signs of women's improved status in Afghan life was Dr. Massouda Jalal's campaign for president in the 2002 *loya jirga* election. The 35-year-old medical professor, who had worked with the World Food Program in Kabul, was the first woman in Afghan history to run for president. She earned the second-highest number of votes, 171, in the election. Dr. Jalal is an eloquent advocate for adult literacy and a strong central government. In many ways she symbolizes the new Afghan woman—strong, outspoken, and unwilling to be shoved into society's shadows ever again.

"I have been thinking about this for 23 years," she said to the delegates about her run for leadership. "When I see our people suffering, dying of poverty, I would always think, what is our way out of these problems? Now the opportunity has come. I am an Afghan woman and I am qualified to be a leader of this country. That is all that matters."

Refugees and Displaced Persons

Millions of people have fled Afghanistan over the past 25 years becoming a large sub-society of Afghan refugees. Many of the poorer, more recent refugees who escaped to Pakistan, Iran, and other bordering nations, have come back following the fall of the Taliban. But many of the middle-class exiles who left during the Soviet years (1979–1988) settled in the west, especially in the United States. Few of the 25,000 to 150,000 Afghan Americans or their children have returned. The loss of these well-educated, talented people has been a tremendous blow to the country.

However, many Afghan Americans have been spurred on by President Hamid Karzai, who, in speeches and personal appearances, has urged them to come back and help rebuild the country. Afghan exiles of every age and expertise are at least considering making the trip. Many have put down roots in America and will not stay in Afghanistan, but the time they spend training others and rebuilding their homeland will be very valuable.

"These people are almost obsessed with moving back, in waves of talent, with their skills—business, entrepreneurial, educational, medical," said former Republican Congressman Dan Ritt, who heads the nonprofit organization Afghanistan America Foundation, whose purpose is to help them return home.

But there are obstacles. Before they go, many Afghan Americans want to be assured the country is secure and safe. Some need financial support to make the trip. Others want to obtain dual citizenship that will allow them to vote in critical, upcoming Afghan elections. But the signs are good that Afghanistan's long lamented "brain drain" may finally be ending.

The Pakistan Problem

In the 1980s and 1990s, nearly one million refugees fled to neighboring Pakistan, a country that Afghanistan has had serious problems with in the past.

Poor relations between the two countries go back to 1947, when Pakistan was formed as a homeland for Indian Muslims and when India gained its independence from Great Britain. Afghan leaders pressured for a "Pashtunistan," a country for Pashtuns living in northern Pakistan. They were rebuffed by the Pakistanis. The issue continued to keep the two countries at odds through the 1970s, especially during the reign of Mohammad Daoud, who tirelessly championed the cause of Pashtustan.

It is still a contentious issue today, but with some surprising twists. For example, while Pakistan was an ally of the United States during the fight against the Taliban and al-Qaeda in 2001, it strongly opposed the possibility that the Northern Alliance, which is predominantly made up of Tajiks, might seize control of the government in Kabul. The Pakistanis wanted the government run by the Pashtuns, an ethnic group widespread within their own country.

Some of the same terrorist problems that still plague Afghanistan are at work in Pakistan. A number of the Taliban's leading spokesmen came out of the militant Islamic movement in northern Pakistan. Now the same region has become a training ground for new Taliban forces. President Pervez Musharraf's attempts to root out these forces have met with little success.

The issue of Pakistani prisoners in Afghanistan has put the two countries at odds as well. Between 1,000 and 2,000 Pakistanis remained in Afghan prisons at the end of 2002. They made up about half of the imprisoned foreign Muslims who were captured by the Northern Alliance after the Taliban's downfall.

Many of these unfortunate men were encouraged to defend the Taliban after September 11 by radical Islamic clerics and mullahs. A large number of them died in the fighting or suffocated in inhumane packing crates while being transported to prison. Many of the survivors claim to be innocent of terrorism and say their only crime was being in the wrong place at the wrong time.

"We are simple, innocent men," says one Pakistani prisoner, farmer Naim Khan. "So why shouldn't we go home?"

President Musharraf asked the same question when he visited Kabul in April 2002. President Karzai said the Pakistanis would be freed as soon as the innocent have been sorted out from the hard-core members of the Taliban and al-Qaeda.

As Afghanistan finds its way in the months and years ahead, its relations with Pakistan, the neighbor country it most resembles, might improve. That depends, however, as much on events in Pakistan as it does on events in Afghanistan.

Al-Qaeda and the Taliban

The Taliban and al-Qaeda were soundly defeated in Afghanistan in November 2001, but they were not eradicated. By the end of 2002, there were disturbing signs that both were still thriving in the remote southern deserts and that al-Qaeda terrorist training camps were beginning to reemerge.

In September 2002, the United States decided that airborne strikes against the terrorists were not effective enough. They deployed more ground troops. The strategy had not produced satisfying results by early 2003. Late in December 2002, members of al-Qaeda launched a night attack in the eastern province of Paktika, near the Pakistan border, killing a U.S. soldier. It was the first U.S. combat death since August of that year. The same day, a military helicopter crashed in Kabul, killing all seven German peacekeepers aboard and two Afghan children on the ground.

"This accident," said German Chancellor Gerhard Schröder, "makes it tragically clear . . . that the army's mission in Afghanistan is a difficult and dangerous operation."

The 5,500 multinational peacekeeping force faces another danger—that of alienating the Afghans that they have pledged to protect. As for the American ground troops that have been sent in, they have become more and more resented by many local people, especially along the Pakistan border where they have been most active in hunting al-Qaeda terrorists. Some officials are urging the United States to send the soldiers home and to increase financial aid instead. They point to the fact that the United States spends $1 billion in military operations a month in Afghanistan and only $25 million on aid in the same time. However, until al-Qaeda is entirely driven from the country and Afghanistan has its own national army, the peacekeepers will probably remain, however unwanted.

The American Presence

Much of the future of Afghanistan depends on a continuing American presence in the country. When the Americans began their war against the Taliban and their terrorist associates in al-Qaeda, the Afghan people welcomed

Despite all of their country's problems, two Afghan boys in a village near Kandahar face the future with bright smiles. This next generation may be Afghanistan's best hope. (Photo courtesy John Otfinoski)

them as liberators. They not only helped to end the Taliban regime, but 22 years of almost continuous warfare.

Despite some dissatisfaction with ground troops, most Afghans still want the United States to stay in their country and help them make the difficult transition from ancient anarchy to modern nationhood. Many, including President Karzai, are convinced that if the Americans abandon this fragile new democracy, the country will quickly fall apart.

To make good on its promise to go the distance in Afghanistan, the United States Congress passed the Afghanistan Freedom Support Act in November 2002, promising a total of $3.3 billion for reconstruction over a period of four years.

But unresolved tensions remain. President Karzai has been pressured by some leaders to get the United States to end its air strikes against the remnants of al-Qaeda in the south, which has led to property damage and some civilian deaths. The uneasy alliance between U.S. forces and the warlords of the Northern Alliance has brought further criticism. At times, the Americans have unwittingly killed innocent Afghans whose only crime was opposing certain warlords who wanted them eliminated. Rogue warlords who threaten security and a central government must be controlled. However, doing so at this early stage is a delicate task both for the Americans and Karzai. To lose their support entirely could plunge the country once again into civil war, something that few Afghans want.

Finally, the United States must be cautious and thoughtful as it make the uneasy transition from a peacekeeping force to a nation-building one. During this transitional period the United States must not feed the Afghans more democracy at one time than they can take. The country cannot achieve complete democracy in the short term. High expectations should be lowered. If they are not, people may become disillusioned and frustrated when further problems arise and may turn back to what President Karzai has called "the way of the gun and the knife."

Early elections could tip the power balance toward the well-armed, and still powerful, warlords and give them control of the country. On the other hand, too much attention to political matters may shift attention away from more pressing matters—such as hunger, health care, jobs for the unemployed, and peace in the streets.

America's commitment to Afghanistan must remain solid, even as other matters gain priority—like the Iraqi War of March and April 2003, which overthrew the dictatorial regime of Saddam Hussein (b. 1937).

Afghanistan's problems, in the long term, are, after all, problems that affect the United States. This was brought dramatically home on September 11, 2001, when al-Qaeda terrorists, some of them trained in Afghanistan, attacked America. The fight against terrorism is intrinsically bound to the fight against poverty, ignorance, intolerance, and injustice. Nowhere are the battle lines more clearly drawn in the world today than in this ancient land and its suffering, but forever hopeful, people.

NOTES

p. 103 "'What else could I do?'" *New York Times*, March 8, 2002, p. A1.

p. 103 "'If you just give away food . . .'" *New York Times*, March 8, 2002, p. A13.

p. 104 "According to Martin Halperin . . ." *New York Times*, February 23, 2002, p. B11.

p. 106 "'We don't do this because we like it . . .'" *New York Times*, May 5, 2002, p. 22.

p. 106 "'We'll help develop a modern infrastructure . . .'" U.S. Department of State web site. Available on-line. URL: http://usinfo.state.gov/regional/nea/sasia/afghan/text/0912roads/htm. Downloaded on January 2, 2003.

p. 107 "'biblical times . . .'" *New York Times*, October 27, 2002, p. 3.

p. 107 "The Taliban have devastated the land . . ." *New York Times*, October 27, 2002, p. 3.

pp. 108–109 "For adult women like me . . ." New York Times, December 2, 2001, p. B4.

p. 109 "'Our life under the Taliban . . .'" Rosemarie Skaine. *The Women of Afghanistan Under the Taliban*. (Jefferson, North Carolina: McFarland & Company, 2002), p. 94.

p. 109 "'We need to create job opportunities . . .'" Interview with Sima Samar, Minister of Women's Affairs. IRINnews.org. Available on-line. URL: http://www.irinnews.org/report.asp? ReportID=19773&SelectRegion=Cetral_Asia&SelectCountry=AFGHANISTA. Downloaded on December 6, 2002.

p. 109 "'It takes time . . .'" Interview with Sima Samar. IRINnews.org. Available on-line. URL: http://www.irinnews.org. Downloaded on December 6, 2002.

p. 110 "'I have been thinking about this . . .'" "Afghan Women Find Political Voice." Eurasia Insight. Eurasianet.org. Available on-line. URL:http://www.eurasianet.org/departments/insight/articles/eav061402ashtml. Downloaded on January 8, 2003.

p. 111 "'These people are almost obsessed . . .'" *New York Times*, February 10, 2002, p. 15.

p. 112 "'We are simple, innocent men . . .'" *New York Times*, August 23, 2002, p. A3.

p. 113 "'This accident makes it tragically clear . . .'" *Connecticut Post*, December 22, 2002, p. A20.

CHRONOLOGY

ca. 100,000 B.C.

First known people inhabit present-day Afghanistan

ca. 4,000 B.C.

The first towns and small cities appear

ca. 1,500 B.C.

The Aryans of Central Asia invade and establish the kingdom of Bactria

540 B.C.

Cyrus the Great of Persia conquers Bactria

522 B.C.

Zoroaster (Zarathustra), founder of Zoroastrian religion, dies in present-day Afghanistan

328 B.C.

Alexander the Great captures the cities of Herat and Kandahar

246 B.C.

The Bactrians revolt and reestablish their kingdom

ca. 1 A.D.

The Kushans conquer Bactria

241
The Sassonids take over much of Afghanistan

741
The Muslims complete their conquest of Afghanistan

998
Mahmud of Ghazna creates the first Afghan Empire

1219
The Mongols led by Genghis Khan sweep across Afghanistan

1370
Tamerlane establishes the Timurid dynasty

1404–1507
Afghanistan experiences its golden age under the Timurids

ca. 1504–1525
Babur establishes the Moghul Empire of India with Kabul as his capital

1709
Chieftain Mirwais Khan revolts against the Persians in Kandahar

1736
Afghan leader Nader Shah becomes king of Persia

1747
Nader Shah is assassinated; Ahmed Khan Sadozai takes power and establishes the Durrani dynasty, declaring an independent Afghan state

1819
A six-year civil war begins

1826
Dost Muhammad Khan emerges as ruler of Afghanistan

1839–42
The First Anglo-Afghan War is fought

1863
Dost Muhammad Khan dies; his son Sher Ali takes power

1878–80
The Second Anglo-Afghan War takes place

1881
Britain agrees to turn over internal control of the country to Abdu Rahamn Khan

1903
The country's first secondary school opens

1914–18
Afghanistan remains neutral during World War I

1919
Habibullah Khan, Afghan king, is assassinated; his son Amanullah Kahn takes power; the Third Anglo-Afghan War ends in complete independence for Afghanistan

1923
Afghanistan's first constitution is adopted under King Amanullah

1928
Tajik bandit chief Bach Saqqao proclaims himself king

1929
Amanullah abdicates and his cousin Muhammad Nader Shah is elected king

1933
Muhammad Nader Shah is assassinated; his son Mohammed Zahir Shah becomes king

1939–45

Afghanistan remains neutral in World War II

1946

Afghanistan is admitted to the United Nations

1947

The new nation of Pakistan closes its borders with Afghanistan

1953

Muhammad Daoud becomes prime minister

1956

An earthquake takes approximately 2,000 lives

1963

King Zahir Shah removes Daoud from power

1964

King Zahir Shah draws up and gets approval for a new constitution; he
declares Afghanistan a constitutional monarchy

1965

Afghan women vote for the first time in national elections

1972

Famine kills thousands of people

1973

Daoud seizes the government in a coup and declares Afghanistan a republic; King Zahir Shah goes into exile

1974

Afghanistan and the Soviet Union sign a 10-year treaty of neutrality and
non-aggression

1978

Leftist military commanders take over the country in the Great April
  Revolution on April 27 and establish the Democratic Republic of
  Afghanistan, a Communist state

1979

December 25: Soviet troops invade Afghanistan
December 27: Amin is killed in a Soviet-led coup; Babrak Karmal takes
  over the government

1979–89

The Soviet-Afghan War takes place

1985

The Islamic Union of Afghan Mujahideen (IUAM) forms to fight the
  Soviets; Mikhail Gorbachev comes to power in the Soviet Union

1986

Gorbachev makes the first withdrawal of Soviet troops from Afghanistan;
  peace negotiations are attempted in Geneva, Switzerland; Karmal is
  replaced as leader by Mohammad Najibullah

1988

The Soviets and Afghans reach a peace agreement on April 14, 1988;
  Osama bin Laden founds his al-Qaeda terrorist organization

1989

The last Soviet troops leave Afghanistan in February

1990

The mujahideen lay siege to Jalalabad for seven months but fail to take
  the city

1992

The mujahideen, led by Ahmad Shah Massoud, take Kabul; Najibullah
  resigns as president; Burkanuddin Rabbani is named interim president
  on June 28 and is elected to a full term in December

1993

The first terrorist attack on the World Trade Center in New York City takes place in February and claims six lives

1994

September: The Taliban take Herat
Rivaling warlords struggle for control of Kabul in a six-month siege; the Taliban seize Kandahar in October

1996

Osama bin Laden sets up his terrorist headquarters in Afghanistan under the auspices of the Taliban
September 5: The Taliban capture Jalalabad
September 27: The Taliban seize Kabul and declare Afghanistan a "completely Islamic state"

1996–2001

The Taliban regime oppresses the people of Afghanistan

1998

February: The Taliban government announces the "disappearance" of Osama bin Laden
March: The United Nations (UN) withdraws its staff from Kandahar
July: Two UN staff members are murdered in Jalalabad

1999

November: The United States and the UN impose trade sanctions on Afghanistan

2000

Seventeen American servicemen are killed in an al-Qaeda attack on the battleship the USS *Cole* in Yemen on October 12

2001

March: The Taliban, despite worldwide protest, destroy two priceless statues of Buddha in the Bamiya Valley, claiming they are idolatrous

September 9: Afghan mujahideen leader Ahmad Shah Massoud is killed by al-Qaeda agents

September 11: Al-Qaeda terrorists kill an estimated 3,000 people in attacks on the World Trade Center in New York and the Pentagon in Washington

October 1: The U.S. attacks Afghanistan to end Taliban rule and destroy Osama bin Laden's al-Qaeda network

November: The Taliban government falls to the combined forces of the United States and the Northern Alliance

December 11: In Bonn, Germany, a charter is drawn to plan the political future of Afghanistan; Hamid Karzai is named interim chairman of the government

2002

January: The United States pledges nearly $300 million in recovery aid

April: Ex-Afghan king Muhammad Zahir Shah returns home after nearly 30 years in exile

June 13: A *loya jirga* elects Karzai president for the next two years

July 6: Vice President Haji Abdul Qadir is assassinated

September 5: President Karzai escapes an assassination attempt in Kandahar; the same day, a car bomb in Kabul kills 30 people; U.S. president Bush pledges $180 million for a road improvement project

November: Four people are killed during two days of violence between protesting Kabul University students and police; a third assassination attempt on Karzai is thwarted; an audio tape of Osama bin Laden is released, convincing many that he is still alive; the U.S. Congress passes the Afghanistan Freedom Support Act promising $3.3 billion in aid over four years

December 21: A U.S. soldier is killed in Paktita province in a gunfire with al-Qaeda remnants; the same day a military helicopter crash in Kabul kills seven German peacekeepers and two Afghan children

2003

January 28: U.S. troops kill at least 18 rebels possibly working for renegade warlord Gulbuddin Hekmatyar in mountain caves in the fiercest battle in Afghanistan in almost a year

January 31: At least 16 Afghans are killed in a minibus when they hit a mine outside Kandahar

February: Germany and the Netherlands take charge of the international peacekeeping force in Kabul; President Karzai visits President Bush at the White House

March: A Red Cross worker from El Salvador is killed by a pro-Taliban group in Southern Afghanistan; the Afghan legislature presents Karzai with a draft of a new national constitution

April 6: A UN-sponsored three-year plan to disarm, demobilize, and reintegrate 100,000 Afghan militiamen is announced

May 1: The United States declares its major combat operations in Afghanistan are over and that international reconstruction efforts can begin in earnest

FURTHER READING

NONFICTION BOOKS

Ali, Sharifah Enayat. *Afghanistan* (New York: Marshall Cavendish, 1995). A volume in the *Cultures of the World* series. An excellent young adult introduction to Afghanistan, especially its people and culture.

Bonner, Arthur. *Among the Afghans* (Durham, N.C.: Duke University Press, 1987). A *New York Times* reporter retells his experiences in Afghanistan in 1985 and 1986 during the Soviet-Afghan War.

Elliot, Jason. *An Unexpected Light: Travels in Afghanistan* (New York: Picador USA, 2001). An Anglo-Afghan writes about his journeys in his homeland in the 1990s. This book could have benefited from an index.

Ewans, Martin. *Afghanistan: A Short History of Its People and Politics* (New York: HarperCollins, 2002). A thorough and concise—if somewhat dry—account of Afghan history that may be hard going for high school students.

Foster, Leila Merrell. *Afghanistan* (New York: Childrens Press, 1996). Another addition to the excellent young adult *Enchantment of the World* series, whose narrative ends before the Taliban era.

Griffin, Michael. *Reaping the Whirlwind: The Taliban Movement in Afghanistan* (Sterling, Va.: Pluto Press, 2001). A good, comprehensive account of the Taliban regime with a useful chronology of events.

Lerner Publications. *Afghanistan . . . In Pictures* (Minneapolis, Minn.: Lerner, 1997). Part of the young adult *Visual Geography* series, slightly outdated now.

Library of Congress. *Afghanistan: A Country Study* (Baton Rouge, La.: Claitor's Publishing Division, 2001). A useful reference work with the most current statistics and other mostly up-to-date information.

Sarin, Maj. Gen. Oleg, and Col. Leo Dvoretsky. *The Afghan Syndrome: The Soviet Union's Vietnam* (Navato, Calif.: Presidio Press, 1993). A somewhat prosaic account of the Soviet-Afghan War by two former officers of the Soviet army.

Skaine, Rosemarie. *The Women of Afghanistan under the Taliban* (Jefferson, N.C.: McFarland & Company, 2002). A compelling report by an American sociologist containing many interviews with Afghan women.

FICTION, PLAYS

Kushner, Tony. *Homebody/Kabul* (New York: Theatre Communications Group, 2002). A play about life in Afghanistan by a Pulitzer Prize–winning playwright.

Rahimi, Atiq, translated from the Dari by Erdag M. Goknar. *Earth and Ashes* (New York: Harcourt, 2002). A gripping novella by a leading Afghan writer. Set during the Soviet-Afghan War.

Shah, Amina. *Tales of Afghanistan* (London: Octagon Press, 1982). A rich anthology of folktales from one of the leading folktale collectors in the world today.

FURTHER VIEWING

Afghanistan, The Vicious Circle. prod. and dir. Nima Sarvestani, National Geographic, VHS, 2001.

Iran & Iraq/Afghanistan. Cpm/Central Park Media, VHS, 2001.

National Geographic—Afghanistan Revealed. National Geographic, VHS, 2001. A solid documentary made mostly before September 11 that includes a close-up profile of the late Northern Alliance commander Ahmad Shah Massoud.

WEBSITES

Afghan Info Center. URL: http://www.afghan-info.com/afghnews.htm. Many news articles, interviews and features. As of January 2003, the site is still under construction and about four months behind in news events.

Afghanland.com URL: http://afghanland.com/home/home.html. Articles, biographies, and features on many subjects and people, particularly good in the arts and entertainment.

AfghanPedia from Sabawoon Online. URL: http://sabawoon.com/afghanpedia/default.shtm. An encyclopedic resource covering a full range of topics on Afghanistan: the land, people, economy, and history. Includes comprehensive daily news reports.

INDEX

Page numbers followed by *m* indicate maps, those followed by *i* indicate illustrations, and those followed by *c* indicate an item in the chronology.